Oral Language for Today's Classroom

CLAIRE STAAB

Pippin Publishing Limited

"A Cone of Experience" from *Audio-Visual Methods in
Teaching*, Third Edition by Edgar Dale, copyright © 1969
by Holt, Rinehart and Winston, Inc., reprinted by permission
of the publisher.

Edited by Dyanne Rivers
Designed by John Zehethofer
Printed and bound by The Alger Press Limited

Canadian Cataloguing in Publication Data

Staab, Claire
    Oral language for today's classroom

(The Pippin teacher's library ; 8)
Includes bibliographical references.
ISBN 0-88751-046-9

1. Oral communication — Study and teaching
(Elementary). 2. Language arts (Elementary).
I. Title. II. Series.

LB1572.S73 1992   372.6'044   C92-093886-8

ISBN 0-88751-046-9

10   9   8   7   6   5   4   3   2   1

CONTENTS

"Doing" Oral Language in the Classroom *107*

Bibliography *120*

. . . .

PREFACE

We chat on the telephone, make appointments and request information, present a financial report to our club, ask the gas station attendant for directions, or tell our children a bedtime story. Throughout the day, we use oral language — speaking and listening — constantly. Our ability to use oral language effectively and appropriately often affects our success in interpersonal relationships as well as business transactions.

A few years ago, I took a case to small claims court and won. The other party decided to appeal and the case went to the Court of Appeals in Vancouver, British Columbia. I immediately contacted a lawyer who informed me that he would charge $130 an hour to prepare the case and at least $1,000 if it went to court. As the dispute involved only $1,800, I decided to represent myself. The other party had hired a lawyer, which meant I would be competing with a professional and responsible for court costs if I lost.

Immediately, I began to make telephone calls to find out what free or relatively inexpensive legal help I could find. Through the lawyers' referral service (lawyers obtained through this service will provide a half-hour's advice for a nominal fee of $10 before negotiating a fee with the client) and the University of British Columbia Law Students Society, I was able to obtain expert advice.

Preparing my questions carefully in advance of the appointments, it took little time to learn what procedures would be required in court, how to subpoena witnesses, what evidence would be admissible, and exactly what I would need to prove.

The total cost of this information was $10. On a trip to the courthouse, I learned which papers needed to be filed and obtained information about how to file them from one of the clerks at the counter.

On the day of the trial, I was extremely nervous (scared to death would be more accurate) as the judge and the opposing lawyer appeared in their black robes. However, my evidence was well prepared, I knew what to expect and was counting on my extensive public speaking experience to help me out. The trial lasted 2½ hours. I called my own witnesses and cross-examined witnesses from the opposing side. When the judge ruled in my favor, I was delighted and somewhat amazed to find I had won.

Reflecting on this experience, I could not help but realize how much my experience and ability to use oral language in a variety of situations affected the outcome. From my first telephone call to the presentation in court, this experience provided me with an invaluable tool.

Language Is Power

Language certainly is power and, as we gain the ability to use language effectively to meet our everyday needs, this power becomes available to us. It is this power that we want to make available to the students in our classrooms. Every student should feel confident that he or she can meet personal needs through telephone calls, face-to-face encounters and when speaking publicly.

Oral language, both talking and listening, is a lifetime activity and probably our most important communication tool. Let's begin now to prepare students for this lifetime activity. As they pass through our classrooms, let's model, explain and demonstrate how oral language can be used effectively in a variety of situations and provide lots of opportunities for practice. We learn language by observing, attempting to use it in various situations, and receiving feedback. The classroom is an ideal environment for encouraging these activities, but they will not happen without planning and effort on our part.

Oral Language Is Important

Before we can turn our classrooms into environments for learning and using language, before we can, in a sense, make the power of language available to students, we must be committed to two basic ideas:

— Oral language is important.
— For many students, using oral language effectively in a variety of situations is not a skill that comes naturally.

If we are not thoroughly committed to these two ideas, we may not encourage much oral language in the classroom. Providing students with many opportunities to talk can be time-consuming and, on occasion, exhausting. When children work together in partners or small groups, the noise level in the room rises and this can be tiring. In a classroom alive with oral language — even productive language — the last bell on Friday afternoon can be a welcome, almost blessed, event.

Apart from the increased noise level, I readily admit that it is easier and definitely faster to tell students something than to invite them to discuss it. When students work in groups, we run into all kinds of problems in organizing and structuring activities to ensure that most of the talk is on task and productive. To put up with these "problems" (by placing the word in quotation marks, I'm not denying that they can be very real), we must be truly committed to the need for and the value of oral language. We must believe that the end result is worth the extra effort.

Even though using it involves extra effort, I am so committed to the belief that oral language is a vital part of every classroom that I hope you will pardon a lapse into sermonizing. I believe that oral language is important, not only as a vital communication tool that empowers us in our daily lives but also as a valuable way to learn. I've heard teachers say, "Stop talking and do your work." But children *are* working when they engage in productive talk. This work may not produce a tangible product to be handed in at the end of the period but it is, in fact, work that has benefits.

Talking and listening to others are among the most important ways we can explore and clarify our thoughts. We may not know exactly what we think about something until we put it into words. Talking helps us sharpen our ideas and come to realize what we already know as well as what we need to know. In this sense, the talking process is analogous to the writing process. If we wish students to think, present original ideas and test what they know, it is vital that we provide time and opportunities for talk. On the other hand, if we wish students only to listen to what we say and parrot our words, then providing extensive time for talk may not be so important.

These ideas are well-illustrated in materials that discuss writing conferences. If, for example, a student asks a teacher for help in finding an ending for a piece of writing, the teacher will encourage her to talk through some possibilities rather than suggest an ending. This may not be the easiest or fastest way to help her, but it is the way that will lead to the most learning.

As we listen to others, we often encounter ideas about and perceptions of the world that are different from our own. As this happens, our own world expands. This is particularly true in classrooms that welcome a large number of students from different cultures. Exposure to new ideas often pushes us to expand the limits of our own understanding as we consider different possibilities. Providing time for students to encounter and listen to different ideas creates a rich atmosphere for learning, particularly when they work with a partner or in small groups. By contrast, if teachers do most of the talking while students listen and then work individually, these opportunities may not be fully realized.

Talking about something, even if it is a list of memorized facts, can also enhance our ability to remember it. As I say something aloud, I am, in fact, rehearsing it and this rehearsal leads to memorization. Just as actors in a play need to say their lines aloud many times before they are committed to memory, talking about something can help students remember it.

Oral Language in the Classroom

It's important to provide many and varied oral language experiences in school, not only to clarify our ideas, expand our world and help us remember things, but also because many students need these experiences to help them discover the power of language. When we encourage the use of oral language in our classrooms, we, as teachers, have two goals — to help students learn content and discover the power of language. The first goal may be realized in a quiet classroom, but the second is doomed to failure in that environment. Even children from language-rich homes may not have had many opportunities to cooperate in a small group, lead a discussion, negotiate desired outcomes with peers, or speak before a large group. These are skills they'll need throughout their lives and we can't assume that they will somehow acquire them naturally or learn them outside school.

To learn skills such as these, modeling, practice and feedback are required. The classroom is an ideal place to provide this. The extra time and planning required to encourage oral language is worth it. It is worth it both in terms of helping students learn the intended content and in helping them discover the power of language. As I mentioned earlier, encouraging the use of oral language is not necessarily easy for teachers. Productive small-group work doesn't just happen. It takes time to restructure the curriculum so that students have many opportunities to speak to different audiences for different purposes. As we set out to do this, we are not beginning an easy task, but we are beginning one that will be valuable for us and the children.

Once we are truly committed to the importance of oral language in the classroom, we can begin to encourage it in many subject areas and aspects of the school day. Oral language is not a subject we teach between 9 and 9:40 a.m., nor is it restricted to activities such as show-and-tell or the oral report in social studies.

Oral language provides a way to learn and discover the power of language that is embedded in every subject and every aspect of the school day. It includes the language used when math partners discuss how they arrived at the answer to a particular problem, when a small group responds orally to a shared poem or a novel, when one member of the class fields questions from the group about a piece of writing that has been shared, when a teacher presents a formal lesson to the class and when a teacher and child chat on the playground.

Using oral language is not something that can be compartmentalized and separated from other activities. Rather, it extends over many situations throughout the school day. Our task is not to add another subject to the curriculum but to restructure the existing curriculum to encourage the use of oral language rather than a steady diet of silence and individual work.

A word of caution — as long as I'm sermonizing, perhaps I should say temperance — is in order. This is not an either-or proposition. Naturally, periods of silence and individual work are appropriate and desirable. Many times throughout the school day, we wish students to be quiet and work individually and, on occasion, they may prefer this themselves. These times may include testing situations, silent reading times or periods when the teacher feels that a break is in order. Some children may need this break more often than others and there should always be physical space in the classroom for quiet, individual work. At other times, the whole class may need to be quiet for periods of time. We don't wish to turn our classrooms into environments where students talk from the moment they arrive until they leave. The point is that, as we become committed to the value of oral language, we will seek opportunities to include constructive talk as a natural part of every curriculum area.

The how-to of this restructuring is the subject of this book. It begins by presenting information about the preliminary work necessary to establish a foundation for this. To ensure that our restructuring is successful, we must encourage a conducive physical and psychological atmosphere in the classroom. This includes establishing rules and routines to ensure that talk is productive rather than disruptive and time-wasting. Successful oral language activities seldom just happen. Careful thought and structuring must go into planning these activities. This foundation includes arranging the furniture to allow for different talk structures (i.e., to accommodate large groups, small groups, partners and quiet work areas) and establishing an atmosphere in which students feel free to express their thoughts and opinions.

After the groundwork has been laid, the curriculum can be adapted to include many talk structures. Instead of requiring students to work quietly in individual situations, many learning experiences can be adapted to include large- and small-group work as well as work with partners. Learning experiences can be structured to elicit productive oral language. The next chapter explains these ideas and provides many examples.

After this, we consider the idea of language functions, the purposes for which students use language. Many linguists believe that children initially learn and use language not for the sake of the language itself but because of what they can do with it. Using language, they can get into the ball game or wheedle another helping of dessert. The common functions for which students use language in school are explained and suggestions for planning different talk structures to elicit these language functions are outlined. In this sense, then, we have an additional factor to consider. As we plan talk structures, we must think about how we can organize these situations to focus on the five common language functions.

Oral language encompasses both speaking and listening. Each of the first three chapters includes information that is as relevant to listening as it is to speaking, but the next chapter is devoted primarily to listening. Listening is often a forgotten or neglected subject because many of us assume that it will happen naturally if students pay attention and don't talk. Students are often told to listen (e.g., "Please be quiet and listen") but seldom are activities planned to help foster this ability or to provide an opportunity to practice. This chapter discusses the skills involved in listening and suggests ideas for instruction and practice.

The book ends with what I've termed my "pull-it-all-together" chapter. What might a program that contains a variety of talk structures used for eliciting a variety of language functions look like? I have encountered three basic methods of organizing classrooms:

— Subjects organized into time blocks.
— Use of a theme that includes many subjects.
— Learning stations or centers.

Many variations on these methods are possible and often they are combined within the context of a single classroom. The final chapter provides examples of how oral language can be introduced into any of these situations. When we make oral language an integral part of all subject areas, we needn't change our basic method of organization; we simply need to change how we structure learning experiences within that method.

Along with the method of organization, we must also consider content. Are we studying ancient Greece, the water cycle or the community? The suggestions included in this chapter are intended only as examples. When planning learning experiences for our classrooms, we will take into account the prescribed curriculum as well as the needs, interests and abilities of the children.

Encouraging oral language in the classroom can be hard work, but it is an enjoyable, exciting and valuable way for students to learn. Remember to start small, enjoy your success and move on to more challenging activities.

If your classroom has been a relatively quiet place with much of the focus on individual work, you may wish to try only one or two ideas until you feel more comfortable. In my experience, we move on when we feel comfortable and see that something we've tried is working. If you're already a successful teacher, you need to see change as worthwhile rather than as something that is being imposed on you. If you're a student teacher or a beginning teacher, it's especially important that you take your time in establishing classroom rules and routines because these provide the foundation for building successful oral language activities. On the other hand, perhaps you have been encouraging students to use oral language and do group work for years. From this vantage point, you may feel more comfortable about rapidly incorporating several ideas. Whatever your circumstances, you need to view oral language activities as productive and worthwhile learning experiences. This is unlikely to happen if your comfort level has been exceeded.

Encouraging oral language in the classroom is a process — not something that can be accomplished in a month or even a year. We need time and patience to reap the harvest. As we help students discover the power of language and make it their own, we need to feel comfortable and successful. Monitor your own feelings and take as much time as you need!

. . . .

CREATING AN ENVIRONMENT

FOR ORAL LANGUAGE

A safe, comfortable and relaxed atmosphere is crucial for the development of productive talk in the classroom. The best-planned, most creative activities won't achieve their purposes unless students feel comfortable expressing their true opinions and risking being wrong. This kind of psychological atmosphere can be fostered only by the teacher.

I remember an incident that happened when I was a college student. As is customary on the first day, each of us provided a brief biographical snippet as a way of getting acquainted. One woman gave her name, then commented that she taught oral language at a local school with a high population of second language learners. The professor immediately remarked, "We don't teach oral language. It's learned."

For the rest of the semester, this student was reluctant to participate and, when she did, was careful to express only the opinions of the professor. She felt safe to comply, but not to think, reason and express her ideas. Productive talk was effectively squelched. If an adult reacts this way, think of how an experience like this is likely to affect children and young adults.

If we, as teachers, are committed to productive talk, we must also be committed to creating an atmosphere in which students feel safe to do so. This is the bottom line; there's no getting around it.

To discover how some teachers successfully create this atmosphere, I've spent many hours observing in classrooms where students engage in productive talk and seem to feel safe. After sifting through my observations and experiences, it appears that these teachers have three things in common.

- They're confident of their ability to manage the class. Rules and routines are established from the first day of school.
- They establish an atmosphere of encouragement and risk-taking.
- The arrangement of furniture and equipment is flexible enough to allow for groupings of different sizes — large, small, partners and individuals.

Establishing Rules and Procedures

Make no mistake, what we're trying to do is establish an atmosphere in which productive talk will flourish as a tool for learning and a means of empowering students. To do this, however, we need to be confident that we have fundamental control of the class.

This confidence is necessary if we are to encourage such talk-filled activities as partners working together, small group activities without the teacher present, student-led meetings and student-led discussion groups. Without it, we're likely to guard our control jealously, fearing things will get out of hand. In situations like this, most classroom communication will flow from teacher to the students, and little will flow between students.

We need control so that we can loan it to the students. Carole Edelsky, who teaches at Arizona State University, has noted that it's best to think of this as "loaning" rather than "giving," because doing so means we can get it back anytime we need it. Indeed, some of our confidence springs from this knowledge.

If basic, underlying control isn't in the hands of the teacher, oral language activities can be chaotic and our comfort level will be exceeded. If this happens and, more important, if we see students "fooling around" and not learning, we're likely to abandon our efforts to encourage productive oral language in the classroom.

When discussing classroom control, it may be helpful to review research carried out during the 1970s and '80s. This may be a helpful guide for student or beginning teachers and serve as a reminder to seasoned veterans.

Be prepared, however. Two decades of research will be summarized in a few paragraphs. Fasten your seat belts, take a deep breath, and let's go.

During the 1970s and '80s, various researchers conducted studies to discover why — and how — some teachers were effective in establishing control of their classrooms. It seems that these teachers were especially proficient in getting control early — from the first day of school. They took time at the beginning of the school year to work on control issues in an attempt to minimize disruptive behavior in the future. They did this in four ways:

- Established rules and procedures that were clearly stated and posted for constant reference.
- Discussed with students the rationale underlying the rules and procedures.
- Discussed the consequences if the rules and procedures were not followed.
- Took time to practice the rules and procedures and provided students with feedback about the practice sessions.

In general, while the rules were specific and brief, they could be applied to behavior in many situations. A good example is, "Listen quietly when others are speaking in front of the class."

Like rules, procedures are expectations for behavior, but they usually apply to a specific activity and are aimed at accomplishing, rather than preventing, something. The steps that are followed when distributing or collecting materials is an example of a procedure.

RULES

It's a good idea to state rules clearly. For example, telling students that they must tidy the room at the end of the school day isn't particularly helpful. A rule like this is unclear and open to interpretation. On the other hand, saying, "At the end of the day, all books are to be reshelved, all paper is to be off the floor, and the board is to be erased unless a 'Save' sign appears," leaves little doubt about what is expected.

Research indicates that it's better to couch rules in positive terms. Rather than saying, "Don't talk when others are speaking," try saying, "We listen when others are speaking."

Whenever possible, it's a good idea to involve students in making the rules and get a commitment that they will be followed. Begin on the first day of school with a discussion of why rules are necessary and write your own rock-bottom rules — those on which you won't budge — on the chalkboard. Ask students if they can think of any other rules that would be helpful. A word of caution — keep the list short. Five or six, including the rock-bottom rules, are enough.

After each rule has been written on the chalkboard and discussed, try to get a unanimous commitment from the class to follow it. If there is a great deal of opposition to a rule and it's relatively unimportant — e.g., No chewing gum in class — you may wish to drop it. However, remind the class that it will be re-established if it poses problems in the future. If a few students oppose a rule, clarify and stress again the reasons for it.

Another helpful strategy is to discuss the list of rules with parents as early in the year as possible. Students will be more likely to accept rules if they are accepted by their families.

After rules have been formulated, preferably on the first day of school, they can be copied onto a permanent wall chart and displayed prominently for future reference.

Rules will, of course, vary from classroom to classroom. Nevertheless, in *Educational Psychology: Theory into Practice*, Robert Slavin suggests that these are rock-bottom.

- Be courteous to others (Listen while others are speaking. Disagree, but respect other's opinions).
- Respect others' property (Ask before using or touching).
- Be on task (Work on assigned work and be where one is supposed to be working).
- During whole-group activities, raise a hand to be recognized.

To these, I would add one final rule.

- Maintain an appropriate level of talk at all times.

By level of talk, I mean volume. It's important that the level of talk be appropriate to the activity. Three levels can be applied to most activities:

- Pindrop: Absolute silence when one can literally hear a pin drop.
- Conversation: Quiet voices used when two people are speaking to each other.
- Discussion: Projection of the voice so that one can be heard by class members sitting several metres away.

The pindrop level applies during silent reading, tests, or perhaps when the teacher and students simply need a respite from a busy day. The conversation level applies when partners are working or during general work times. Voices should not be so loud as to disturb others or prevent an individual from working alone. The discussion level applies when small or large groups are working and it's important for several others to hear.

In primary and lower intermediate classes, you may wish to color code (e.g., red for pin drop, yellow for conversation and green for discussion) these talk levels and place an appropriately colored piece of construction paper on a corner of the chalkboard as a reminder during the first few weeks of school.

PROCEDURES

Procedures, too, should be thoroughly explained and demonstrated. While they need not be recorded in writing, they should be practiced extensively. While all procedures can't be formulated on the first day, they should be put into practice as needed within the first few days or weeks.

Some situations crop up regularly in classrooms. The chart on the following page, prepared by Carolyn Evertson and Edmund Emmer, lists some of these, along with procedures some teachers have found effective when dealing with them. Feel free, however, to devise procedures that you and the students can be comfortable with. For example, a student teacher in one of my classes found it offensive that her textbook suggested snapping one's fingers to get students' attention. I agree that this is, or could be, offensive and, besides, I'm not sure that students could hear a finger snapping in a busy classroom. However, even if a particular method is offensive, it doesn't eliminate the need to find an appropriate way to get students' attention.

Situation	Procedure
Getting students' attention.	Blink lights. Ring bell.
Obtaining, handling and replacing materials.	Finished work to be put in red basket.
Lateness.	Obtain pass from office, enter quietly, place pass on teacher's desk.
Entering the classroom.	Quietly. Begin reading.
Dismissal before recess.	Desks clear. Sit quietly.
Public address announcements.	Freeze. No talking. Listen.
Fire drill.	No talking. Line up in single file at rear door.

CONSEQUENCES

Discuss the consequences of violating rules ahead of time so that there are no surprises for students. Be prepared to follow through with these consequences.

In *Comprehensive Classroom Management: Creating Positive Learning Environments*, Vernon Jones and Louise Jones suggest using the following consequences in sequence. The less disruptive a consequence the better, as the objective is to interrupt the flow of instruction or activity as little as possible.

Consequence	Example
Nonverbal cue.	Eye contact. Raised index finger
Verbal cue.	"Sue, check the rules."
Focus on rule.	"Sue, what rule are you violating?"
Student goes to designated area to make plan for following rule and prepare to talk to teacher.	"Sue, take time out to develop your plan."
Student leaves room to make plan — conference with principal, possibly sent home.	"Sue, please see Ms. Johnson."

Rules and procedures need to be practiced until they're automatic. Some classes may need only an explanation and a few practices, while others need more. Time spent doing this at the beginning of the year will be more than repaid by the time saved later. When rules and routines become automatic, we gain the confidence necessary to try new and exciting activities as well as freedom from the burden of constantly imposing discipline. As we all know, this is tiring and robs us of the joy of teaching!

The research mentioned earlier found that effective teachers introduced the rules and many of the classroom procedures on the first day of school. On average, they reviewed or practiced these every day for the first week, three times during the second week, and once a week or whenever the need arose until the end of the first month.

To practice the pindrop level of talk, for example, try inviting the children to be so quiet that you can actually hear a real pin drop. The conversation level, on the other hand, needs to be practiced again and again so that students have a real sense of the degree of noise involved. Students also need to practice being in the midst of conversation or discussion when the teacher gives the signal to pay attention. Students should stop talking within two or three seconds and give the teacher their full attention. This may need to be practiced many times until it can be accomplished within the time limit.

Once rules and procedures are automatic and we're confident that they will be followed, we can begin loaning control to the students as we introduce creative oral activities. In his book, *Classroom Control*, David Fontana notes that insecurities about their ability to control a class loom large in the minds of many inexperienced — and even some experienced — teachers. Establishing and practicing rules and routines will not eliminate these insecurities entirely, but it is a big step towards building the confidence needed to develop an exciting, vibrant program.

The Classroom Atmosphere

Establishing a psychological environment in which children feel valued and ready to take risks is essential for initiating and maintaining successful and productive talk in the classroom. Many experienced teachers are able to establish this atmosphere almost unconsciously at the beginning of the school year. For beginning teachers or those who notice that students seem to be complying rather than stretching their thinking, it may be worth thinking about the factors involved in establishing this atmosphere.

DISPLAY ACCEPTANCE AND TRUST TOWARDS STUDENTS

Children and adults are more inclined to participate and contribute original ideas when they feel secure and valued rather than judged and required to prove themselves continually according to predetermined standards. When we feel accepted for who we are, we're comfortable about being part of the classroom community.

One way to promote an atmosphere of acceptance and trust is to encourage students to express their opinions. Although most teachers agree in principle that students should be invited to express their opinions, research indicates that this is not a reality in many classrooms. In *Analyzing Teacher Behavior*, Ned Flanders reported that teachers talk more than all the students in the class combined by a margin of about three to two. Further, only about three per cent of all teachers' talk involves encouraging students or reacting to their opinions. This condition is nearly as true today as it was 30 years ago when Flanders conducted his studies.

When this happens consistently in the classroom, students' expectations may be affected. If we don't actively encourage them to express opinions, students may pick up on our expectations and cease to believe that their job is to think. They may simply tell us what we want to hear. If talk focuses on things like eliciting facts and expressing the "right" interpretation, students may feel insecure about using it to foster learning. As they progress through the grades, they will begin to assume that school is not an appropriate forum for expressing opinions and thinking creatively.

In today's busy classrooms, teachers know that there are times when explaining procedures or eliciting facts is necessary. Inviting students to express their opinions may not be appropriate when explaining a fire drill procedure or eliciting answers to multiplication questions. At the same time, however, we must strive to find time to ask open-ended questions and encourage the expression of diverse opinions.

In an article that appeared in *Research in the Teaching of English*, Maryann Eeds and Deborah Wells suggest that literature-response groups provide an excellent means for encouraging students to express opinions. As we circulate among these groups, we can ask open-ended questions and make comments such as, "I hadn't thought of that," "Tell me more about your ideas," and "Let's think about that."

We also need to encourage students to trust themselves. In a grade one class where I am a frequent visitor, I arrived one morning to find the teacher and class responding orally to mathematical word problems. The group was led by a child. When the child called on the teacher to give her answer, she responded, then remarked, "Who has a different suggestion? I may be wrong, you know. You need to trust yourself. Remember Christopher Columbus who thought the earth was round when everyone else thought it was flat."

Although answers to the problem were subsequently explained and clarified, the teacher believed it was important to encourage the children to speculate and think creatively without fear of censure by either her or classmates.

Students also need permission to admit uncertainty. We don't always have to know an answer and sometimes our uncertainty becomes the basis for important learning. Eavesdropping on a grade two classroom, we see a teacher working with children to explore whether numbers are odd or even. When a difference of opinion arises among students, the teacher asks, "How many think it's even? Raise your hands." "How many think it's odd? Raise your hands." "How many really don't know?" When one child raises his hand, the teacher comments, "What an honest person," then helps the children find the solution.

Even in a situation like this, where there is a single correct answer, the teacher attempted to communicate to the children that admitting uncertainty is not only all right but also honest. It's important for the teacher to model admitting uncertainty to show the students that it really is all right to be unsure.

Let's imagine a grade four teacher working with a child during a writing conference. The child asks how to spell "laryngitis." The teacher freely admits, "I don't know how to spell that word — I'll have to look it up in the dictionary. Shall we do that together?" If the teacher can admit uncertainty, it may help children feel secure about owning up to the fact that they don't know.

LISTEN TO STUDENTS

In addition to displaying acceptance and trust, truly listening to students is another major factor in establishing a supportive psychological atmosphere. All of us feel more disposed to talk when we believe someone is really listening and students are no exception.

Picture yourself at a social gathering. As you are talking to someone, that person is looking around the room, watching other people. How would you react? If the person offered no explanation, I would feel that I wasn't very important to that person and would probably excuse myself as soon as possible.

Do we do this to students in the classroom, not because we're not interested in them but because we simply have so many things to do? How do students interpret this fracturing of attention? Do they feel unimportant?

In busy classrooms, there are certainly times when we can't listen attentively to individual students. Nevertheless, we must communicate this in a way that indicates that we are interested in what they have to say.

In a grade one classroom I recently visited, the teacher responded to children who approached her to talk either by saying, "I'm not able to discuss that right now. We'll talk later," or by giving them her undivided attention, including constant eye contact.

The teacher did not half concentrate on what a child was saying while looking around the room to make sure the rest of the class was behaving. The child received the message — you are important enough to receive my undivided attention.

To give individuals our undivided attention, we must be confident that the other children will go about their business without constant supervision. This is another important reason for establishing rules and procedures at the beginning of the school year. Freed from the need to monitor discipline constantly, we can devote more time to observing and listening to students.

It's worth noting that we should try to avoid interrupting our conversations with children — for other teachers or even the principal. I feel very strongly that our undivided attention says to each child, "I value you. You matter. You're a vital part of this classroom. As I give you my undivided attention even for a few moments, I'm letting you know that you are important."

VALUE STUDENTS EQUALLY

In addition to showing children that we value them by listening carefully when they speak, it's important to show them that we value all students equally. Classrooms in which some children are considered "screaming eagles" and others "mud ducks" do not provide a supportive atmosphere for all students.

In the grade one classroom described previously, it's obvious that the contributions of all the children are valued equally. During reading period, they choose their own library books and decide whether they wish to read with a partner. During my last visit, one group of three children spontaneously chose to work out a choral reading, one group of two prepared a flannelboard presentation and several partners engaged in buddy reading of fairly long books.

After this half-hour period, the teacher asked whether anyone would like to share a story with the whole class and several children volunteered. Both the teacher and the other children commended the readers, whether their contributions were a single line from a simple story or a cleverly assembled choral reading of several pages. All those who shared their stories felt comfortable, secure and appreciated.

RESPECT STUDENTS' FEELINGS

How often I have thought that because I'm feeling a certain way, everyone else must be feeling the same! Over the years, I've learned that it's probably a good idea to check out how others are feeling rather than make assumptions. Fortunately, many teachers do just that — check out how students are feeling and respect those feelings. This certainly helps create the atmosphere we're looking for.

Let's look in on a grade three classroom this time. The children are holding a brainstorming session to come up with a list of different kinds of monsters and the teacher is recording their suggestions on the chalkboard.

John calls out, "A scary monster," and Peter adds, "A hairy monster." Then Kim pipes up, "A Jill monster."

One child in the room is named Jill. The teacher immediately stops and asks her, "How do you feel about that? Do you want to leave it up or take it down?"

Jill decides that she likes it and wants to leave it on the chalkboard. The teacher respects Jill and her feelings enough to let her decide and Jill feels secure enough to share her feelings. In the same circumstances, I'm sure I would have been very hurt, but this teacher didn't automatically assume that this was the case. She took time to check out Jill's feelings.

Here's another example, from my own experience. Although it happened several years ago when my son was in grade eight, it's still very fresh in my mind. One day he came home from school extremely upset and told me that his English teacher had called him a clod. After this happened several times over the next few days, I became very disturbed and made an appointment to see the teacher. Needless to say, I went to the conference loaded for bear.

I had never met this teacher and was completely unprepared for what I found. Here was an extremely delightful, interesting woman, not at all the ogre I'd expected. In response to my question about calling my son a clod, she said with a laugh, "Oh, yes, I call all the boys clods and the girls clodettes. That's just the way they are at this age."

Even though she meant no harm and was certainly not the kind of person who would knowingly hurt students, she had caused harm because she hadn't bothered to check out how they felt.

In most classrooms I visit, this notion of respecting the feelings of others is a common thread. In a grade three class, for example, the rules are simple and direct.

- We don't have the right to hurt another's feelings.
- We don't touch others' possessions without their permission.
- We clean up our own mess because the room belongs to all of us.

From the first day of school, the teacher focuses on these ideas. On one occasion, she returned to school after a three-day absence and found the classroom quite messy. She gathered the class together and said, "It bothers me that I was away and the room is now a mess."

Notice the she shared her own feelings, using "I" statements, instead of trying to assign blame or reprimand the children. Afterwards, she focused on what had happened and how the situation could be fixed, not on who did it. She was willing to share her feelings and participate with the children in attempting to find a solution. She expected students to respect her feelings, just as she respected theirs.

SHIFT CONTROL TO STUDENTS

In an article included in *Whole Language: Theory in Use,* Judith Newman wrote that knowledge is not something that exists apart from students. Rather it is something students are actively engaged in creating as they seek to know, to understand, and to make sense of their world. If students are to engage actively in seeking knowledge, some of the responsibility for learning must be theirs. To help them assume this responsibility, teachers must take steps to shift control to them.

Once classroom control is established, I've observed that effective teachers shift this control to students by believing that all of them are capable, by offering them choices, and by giving them increased responsibilities. This doesn't mean that teachers completely abdicate responsibility. Students are not asked, for example, if they would like to substitute extra reading for math, leave assignments incomplete, or plan the year's curriculum in science. Neither are they asked to teach lessons on a regular basis or assume the primary responsibility for evaluating their progress. Nevertheless, we need to believe that they are all capable and search for opportunities, whenever possible, to offer them responsibility and freedom of choice.

BELIEVE ALL STUDENTS ARE CAPABLE

The fundamental belief that all students are capable can be summed up by the following statements:

- Students know...
- Students can...
- I trust that students will...

Every child knows things and can operate successfully on some level. It's our responsibility to discover what each child already knows and facilitate progress. The teacher is positive, positive, positive — not in a superficial way by heaping on insincere praise but in a way that helps the child feel successful.

I smile every time I visit a particular ungraded primary classroom because the children always tell me how clever they are. They do this because the teacher believes it to be true and tells them so.

For example, a six-year-old brought a page containing a picture and four letters to the teacher. The teacher said sincerely, "Wonderful. I'd really like to know more about your picture. Will you tell me about it?"

The teacher didn't criticize the writing because she recognizes that the construction of meaning through writing is a series of successive approximations and that this child had been successful.

Let's eavesdrop now on a grade seven class where Sean is sharing a piece of writing with the teacher and three other students during a group writing conference. He reads his story about a young boy who lives with his grandfather. The grandfather dies suddenly and Sean can't decide whether to end the story by having the boy die too so he can find his grandfather in the afterlife or by having the boy find a friend to share his troubles with.

The teacher asks Sean to talk through both endings and then says, "I like both your ideas, Sean. Either one would make a good ending, but I think you need to work that out for yourself. I think you're stuck because you're having trouble choosing among so many good ideas, but you'll work out how best to end the story." Notice that her statement emphasized the ideas, you know..., you can..., and I know you will....

In a grade four classroom, students are working in pairs to make up and solve their own word problems. One child comes to the teacher and asks, "Does that equal 75?" The teacher asks, "What does your partner think? Try to work it out between the two of you."

After three or four similar requests from other pairs, the teacher blinks the lights, his signal for quiet, and begins to brainstorm with the children about the strategies that can be used if partners disagree on an answer. The following strategies are developed and recorded on the chalkboard:

— Try it again.
— Get manipulatives and count.
— Talk it over with your partner and explain how you got the answer.

When one child points out that manipulatives don't work very well if there are too many items, they decide that the problem-solving technique selected may depend on the problem. The teacher then sums up the brainstorming session with the comment, "Come to me only as a last resort. Do all the things you've just thought of first." He is not withdrawing support from the children, but is simply pointing out that he is confident that they can complete the task.

During newstime in a grade six classroom, one boy brings in an item regarding the Mohawk blockade in Oka, Quebec. Another boy has a conflicting report and the students begin to argue. The teacher uses this as an opportunity to explore with the class some reasons for the conflicting reports and discrepancies in information. They talk about what each student might do to get further information to prove his point. The students are then invited to work through the problem and bring in further news the following day. The teacher is confident that the students can solve this dilemma because she believes that helping them develop effective learning strategies is more important than finding a speedy answer to the question.

Effective teachers also encourage children to work out personal conflicts between themselves whenever possible. In a grade two classroom, a student comes to the teacher to complain, "Margaret has had two turns and I haven't had any." The teacher suggests, "Go back and tell Margaret what you've just told me and see if the two of you can come to an agreement." Later in the day, another child comes to him, saying, "I have a problem. You said both Danielle and I could be first today." He responds, "Okay, how could we work this out?" This teacher believes that students can get along together and solve their own interpersonal problems.

In all the preceding examples, the teachers believe themselves to be the last resort rather than the supreme authority. By means of brainstorming, class meetings and informal discussions, students develop skills and guidelines for dealing with interpersonal problems. If students are offered the tools and the opportunity, these teachers believe them capable of solving problems.

OFFER CHOICES

In all the classrooms I visit, the teachers seek opportunities to provide students with choices. For example, students often choose their own books for reading period, their own topics during writing time, their own partners for buddy reading and the members of their small groups for discussions.

In one intermediate learning assistance center, students are offered the choice of putting a library book back on the shelf and choosing another. As we enter this classroom, one student is obviously struggling with a particular book. After the teacher works with him to develop a strategy for deciding when a book is too difficult, the decision to keep or replace the book is left to him. The teacher comments, "The most important thing about reading is that you enjoy it." The teacher doesn't say, "That book is too hard for you. You need to put it back and choose another."

The school day provides many opportunities for offering students choices. These can even extend to some housekeeping chores. For example, a grade two teacher places a stack of papers on each child's desk and asks the children to pass them out later in the day when time permits. At recess, she comments, "You may continue to pass out the papers at recess or give them back to me."

OFFER STUDENTS RESPONSIBILITY

Whenever possible, effective teachers offer students responsibility for handling classroom procedures. The message is that this is our room and our class and we're all here together to learn and grow in every way we can.

In a grade one classroom, for example, a six-year-old boy handles a five-minute transition between activities without the teacher's intervention. As the teacher begins to prepare for math period by placing manipulatives on the children's desks, she asks Joshua to teach the class a new song he has learned. Joshua sings the song and encourages the class to repeat the words line by line, then monitors as the class sings. Of course, the teacher has modeled this procedure many times. Once children are familiar with it, they're encouraged to lead the group.

In some classrooms, teachers have introduced a practice called teacher of the day. Each day, one child is chosen to lead the morning exercises, which normally consist of calling the roll, doing the calendar and completing the weather chart. By Christmas, this routine is highly successful, even in grade one classrooms. In one grade one class, for example, the teacher of the day leads a short game that involves the children in clapping while reciting the days of the week and snapping their fingers while reciting the months of the year. At the suggestion of the children, the game can be changed to, for example, hopping the days of the week and clapping the months of the year.

The teacher of the day may also have other duties. In many primary classrooms, children are honored on their birthdays. In one classroom, it is the teacher of the day's responsibility to make this presentation. Throughout the day, the "teacher" is also responsible for assisting in other ways, such as dismissing children at appropriate times, moderating sharing times and helping with the collection and distribution of materials.

Students are also encouraged to take responsibility for maintaining the classroom. In one primary class, I was playing a board game on the floor with three children. I finished and prepared to leave, but they wished to continue. One of them remarked politely, "We all have to pick up whatever we use." Embarrassed, I replaced my playing pieces in the box.

ASSESSING OUR SUCCESS

Establishing a psychological environment conducive to using oral language successfully is simple, yet difficult. It's difficult in that there are no specific activities that can be readily outlined and prescribed. Rather, it requires a shift in attitude that must be nurtured until it becomes automatic.

Fundamental to establishing this attitude is a belief in the value of oral language and children's innate capabilities. It bears repeating that before this attitude can be established — and, particularly, before control can be shifted to the students — the rules and procedures discussed earlier must be firmly established.

I'm including an assessment tool that may prove useful for some teachers until this attitude becomes automatic. The components of a supportive psychological atmosphere are condensed into four main headings: Encourage Student Opinion, Listen to Students, Value Students Equally and Shift Control to Students. Record plans for helping these things happen under Plans and, until clear evidence of each is noted, record anecdotal notes stating what happened under Evidence.

For example, under plans for shifting control to students, a teacher may write, "Start training children to take over sharing time." As the week progresses, the teacher may record under evidence, "Student helper taking roll."

Assessment of Psychological Atmosphere

Month_____ Year_____

Week 1	Week 2
Encourage Student Opinion	
Plans	Plans
Evidence	Evidence
Listen to Students	
Plans	Plans
Evidence	Evidence
Value Students Equally	
Plans	Plans
Evidence	Evidence
Shift Control to Students	
Plans	Plans
Evidence	Evidence

The Physical Environment

If teachers are to create a physical environment conducive to productive talk, two issues are paramount:

— The arrangement of furniture and equipment must allow for flexibility in grouping.
— There must be interesting content to stimulate talk.

Productive talk doesn't just happen, it is planned for and facilitated.

ARRANGE FURNITURE FOR FLEXIBILITY

While none of the teachers whose classrooms I visit places desks in straight rows, this is certainly possible if the desks can be moved easily. In most rooms, students are seated at tables or desks are arranged in small clusters. This clustering makes it easy for children to talk softly to one another during work time and means that teachers can rely on students to help each other. In primary classrooms particularly, children are encouraged to obtain help from others in spelling, reading and other tasks. Certainly, there are times, such as during tests or when someone is reading aloud or speaking to the group, when silence is the rule, but generally children are encouraged to interact with one another.

Individual desks arranged in straight rows make this interaction more difficult — and noisier — because students are farther apart. Because students normally do not remain in their desks during large-group gatherings, it often doesn't matter if desks are placed so that everyone can see the chalkboard or the front of the room.

Most teachers designate a large open space, usually in the front of the chalkboard, for use as a gathering place. In primary classrooms, this area is often covered with a rug. In this area, whole-class lessons are taught, class meetings are held, and students present plays and reports or participate in sharing times.

Various small-group areas are also set up around the room. These often include a round table where five or six children can gather or they may simply be open areas where children can bring their own chairs or sit on the floor. In primary classrooms, children often use these spaces to play a game with two or three others or put together a puzzle with a partner. Small-group discussions, group planning and peer conferences take place in these areas. In her book, *In the Middle: Writing, Reading and Learning with Adolescents*, Nancie Atwell describes areas in her grade eight classroom that are reserved for these kinds of activities. Students may use them for no other purpose and class members must respect the privacy of students who are engaged in peer conferences in these areas.

Included in these small group areas are interest centers, such as a library center, a game or math manipulatives center, a science center, a book publishing and writer's supply center and, in primary classrooms, often an art or painting center. The number and kind of interest centers will vary with the needs of the children. Some may change often while others, such as the library center, are virtually permanent.

Teachers also make provision for students who need or want to work alone with relatively little interruption. In primary classrooms, I often observe small cubby holes, perhaps behind a piece of furniture, where a child can be alone with a book or piece of writing. In intermediate classrooms, individual desks or small tables are often set in a quiet area of the classroom that can serve the same purpose.

The exact arrangement of furniture is unimportant, as the key is to allow for maximum flexibility in grouping — large, small, partners and individuals — without the inconvenience of moving furniture. The diagrams on the following pages illustrate arrangements that have worked well in primary and intermediate classrooms.

CREATE INTERESTING CONTENT

Students don't talk about talk. They talk about what's happening in their world — their home, their outside activities, their classroom. As teachers, we have little control over what happens to children outside school, but we do have control over what happens in the classroom and this is a large part of any student's day. We must ask ourselves what's happening in our classrooms. Are they interesting places to be? Can students be involved in classroom activities and find something to think, talk or write about? As you look around your classroom, ask yourself two questions:

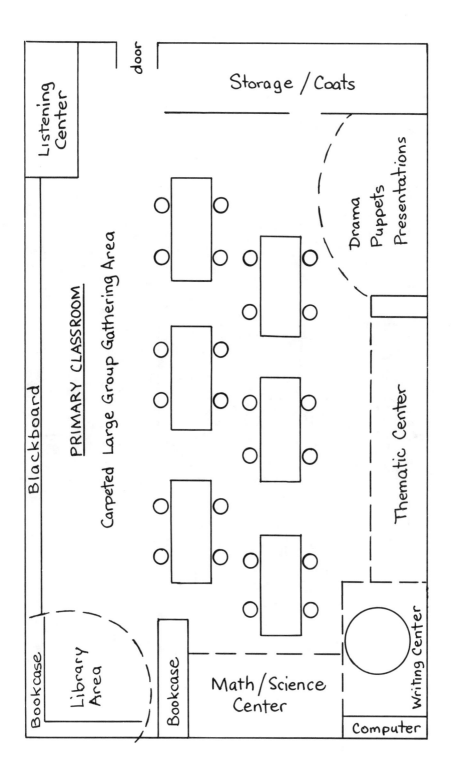

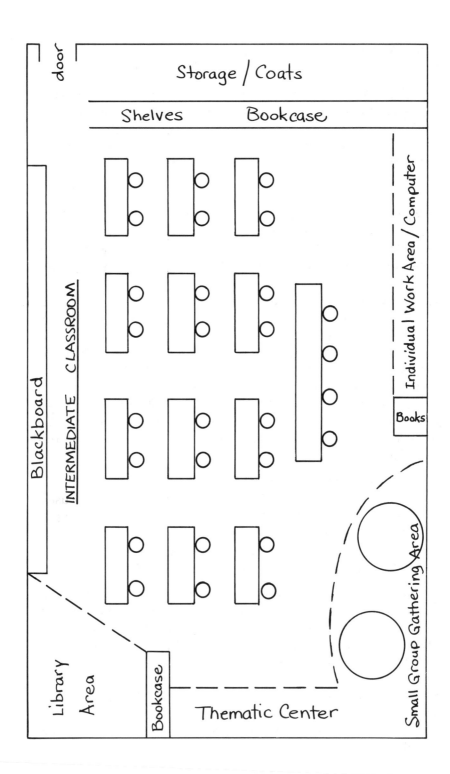

- Do I find this a stimulating place?
- Am I anxious to come to school each day?

If the answer to either question is no, some of the following suggestions may help your classroom become a more interesting place — for you and the students. These suggestions are merely starting points. Ideally, interesting content flows from the curriculum and students' own interests.

Collections

Bringing your own personal collections to the classroom is an excellent way to create a more interesting environment, encourage research and library skills, and shift control to the students. Begin by bringing in articles that you actually collect. This might include coins, stamps or, in my case, a set of antique kitchen utensils. If you don't have a genuine collection or if it is too valuable to bring into the classroom, an interesting collection can be devised easily. For example, you might gather various seeds, species of bugs, or types of buttons or fasteners. The collection could be almost anything that shares a common attribute.

The collection should be arranged on a table. During whole-group sharing time, you can talk about it and invite the children to ask questions. This discussion might cover the following:

- What is the collection (unless it's obvious)?
- Label and tell a little bit about each item. What is it used for? Where did I get each item? Why did I choose to put each item in my collection?
- Why are these items being collected?
- How do I plan to add to the collection?

The class is then responsible for generating a list of questions that haven't yet been answered. Class members take responsibility for consulting reference materials or other resources to discover the answers and report back to the class.

A collection may remain on display for a few days or several weeks, depending on interest. Ideally, collections will relate to a topic under study. For example, my collection of antique kitchen utensils is appropriate for a unit on pioneer life.

After the teacher has modeled presenting two or three collections and established the procedures for this activity, students are invited to present collections of their own. This shifts control because a student now becomes the expert on a particular subject. This can be a real learning experience for the teacher, as I found a few years ago in Powell River, British Columbia, when a grade four student presented a collection of fishing lures. Both my knowledge and my vocabulary increased immensely thanks to his presentation.

News Bulletin Boards

In intermediate classrooms especially, it's a good idea to devote a bulletin board to articles about a news event. It's best to follow only one major story at a time — one in which students express interest.

Invite students to search newspapers and magazines, listen to radio reports and watch TV so they're prepared to report events on a daily basis as they unfold. This gives the students an opportunity to tell what's new each day, and often motivates the writing of letters to government officials or invitations and thank-you letters to guest speakers.

Pets and Plants

Pets can be a nuisance in the classroom if they're ignored as a learning tool. Feeding them and cleaning up the mess can become a real chore. However, if used wisely, pets can stimulate a variety of interesting activities. For example, fish in an aquarium can be carefully observed to note the parts of the body used for swimming, how they feed, what the best environment is for various fish, and which species do well in the same aquarium. This information can be gathered through research and observation and is a subject for talk.

In the same way, plants can be grown from seeds and tested for growth under different light and moisture conditions. As students check these plants daily, perhaps recording their findings in log books, talk is stimulated.

Penpals

Establishing a penpal with another student the same age can be a great motivator for writing activities. If the penpals are in the same district, several letters a week can be enclosed in one large envelope and sent free of charge through the school board's courier. If a computer system with a modem is in place, students can write their letters on the computer and send them directly to the penpal at another school.

If all the students have a mailbox in the classroom, they find it very exciting to arrive each morning, check the mailbox, and find a letter from a penpal. Writing these letters is an excellent authentic writing activity and can also provide something for students to do when work is finished. If possible, at the end of the year, the two classes can gather at a park for a picnic so that penpals can meet each other.

Festivals and Special Occasions

Halloween, Christmas and Hanukkah are probably mentioned in most classrooms. Why not celebrate other holidays like St.David's Day and Chinese New Year? In her book, *Let's Celebrate: Canada's Special Days*, Caroline Parry describes more than 100 holidays celebrated by ethnic groups in Canada. Celebrating some of these in the classroom can spark activities like inviting guests from a particular ethnic community, examining multicultural literature, making traditional foods, displaying items representative of a particular culture, and learning traditional dances or songs.

Field Trips, Excursions and Guest Speakers

As administrators cut back on finances, teachers are often allowed only one or two field trips a year. What a shame! A well-planned field trip can be a very worthwhile experience.

Even with financial restraints, however, it is often possible to take additional trips. For example, the class might take a fall walk to collect different colors and varieties of leaves or a walk to explore the architecture of neighboring buildings. With the help of parents, it may be possible to take a city bus to visit more distant locations.

Teachers can spend a few worthwhile hours contacting the community's chamber of commerce, tourism bureau and other organizations to find out what's of interest in the community. Better yet, teachers may invite students to make these inquiries themselves early in the school year.

In some communities, little theaters, children's theaters, and opera and dance companies will allow school classes to attend dress rehearsals free of charge. If the presentation is appropriate for a particular age group, this can be an enriching experience for students who might not otherwise have an opportunity to attend.

At the beginning of the school year, it's also a good idea to poll parents on their hobbies and interests. Often a parent makes a very interesting guest speaker. This is particularly true if you're lucky enough to teach in a multicultural class-room.

TALK STRUCTURES

The stage is set. We've rearranged the furniture in our classrooms to create interest centers and established rules and routines that students are following regularly. We're well on our way to creating an atmosphere in which students are offered more choice and control and feel free to take risks. We're now ready to plan activities that encourage productive talk.

Let's imagine that it's a beautiful fall day. A grade four teacher has provided each of the children in his class with a paper bag and invited them to collect unusual and beautiful leaves from the playground. The teacher, too, makes a collection. Afterwards, the children return to the classroom and empty their bags onto their desktops. The teacher empties his own bag onto a small table at the front of the room and the scenario continues:

Teacher: I've collected some really interesting leaves. Let's look at some of the beautiful colors. I have one that is amber (holds up a leaf) which is a kind of yellow-brown. If you have an amber leaf, would you hold it up?

Several children hold up leaves.

Teacher: Another one I think is beautiful is a kind of vermilion shade, which is this beautiful reddish-orange color. Who has one?

Two children hold up leaves.

Teacher: Here's a different one. It's maroon. How about that color?

Again, several children hold up leaves.

Teacher: Here's one I'd call chartreuse. What colors seem to blend together to make chartreuse? (Pause) Elaine?

Elaine: It looks like yellow and green.

Teacher: Yes, I agree. Do any of you have other colors?

Sarah: Here's one that's yellow, but not really.

Teacher: What would we call that? (Pause) Paul?

Paul: A dark yellow.

Teacher: Parts of it certainly are. To me, it seems like a dappled or mottled yellow because of the dark spots on it. We might even use another word, "variegated," to describe the different shades of yellow. What about this leaf? Do you notice anything different about it? (Pause) Latoya?

Latoya: It's very thin. I can see lines in it and the light behind it.

Teacher: What do we call these lines?

No one responds.

Teacher: These lines are called veins and, yes, we can see the light behind it so we could say it's translucent. It lets some light shine through it. Can you find a leaf that either has veins or is translucent?

Several children hold up leaves.

Teacher: (Holding up two dead leaves) What about these? How could we describe them?

Ho Lun: Dead.

Peter: Brown.

Teacher: Yes, that's absolutely right and we might also use the words, "withered" and "parched." Why do you suppose these leaves look like this while some of the others are so colorful? (Pause) John?

John: Those have been on the ground longer.

Teacher: Possibly. Najma?

Najma: They're older.

Teacher: That could be very true, but why do they lose their color?

Andrew: They need water.

Teacher: Yes, that's so. They've lost all their moisture and without moisture, living plants turn brown. What questions do you have about the dead leaves or anything else we've looked at?

After discussing the children's questions, the teacher and children go on to identify common varieties of leaves, such as oak and maple. Afterwards, the children are invited to list in writing words or phrases that provide information about leaves. Labeled pictures and other reference materials are available for those who choose to use them. During this period, the teacher functions as a resource, answering children's questions and providing further vocabulary and ideas to individuals. Then, the children explain to a partner why they included each word or phrase on their list.

The next day, the children form groups of three or four. Combining the contents of their bags, they decide jointly on a plan for dividing their leaves into categories — by color, size, variety, etc. The leaves in the category are then pasted on a large sheet of paper, which is labeled and presented to the class. Group members explain the category they chose and other students are encouraged to ask questions. These category charts can be used to create a class bulletin board or displayed at the science center.

These activities demonstrate how a variety of talk structures — opportunities for children to relate to audiences of different sizes and types — can encourage learning. They encompass the range of talk structures available in elementary school classrooms:

- Teacher-to-large or small groups.
- Child-to-adult.
- Child-to-child (partner).
- Child-to-small group.
- Child-to-large group.

If we have created a conducive psychological and physical environment and taken time to establish clear rules and procedures, we should feel comfortable encouraging students to use a variety of talk structures. If we have not gained control over the class so that we don't feel comfortable loaning this control to students, it's likely that the talk structures in our classrooms will be mostly teacher-to-child or teacher-to-small and large groups. Teachers who haven't taken time to establish clear-cut rules may feel uncomfortable with child-to-child, child-to-small group and even child-to-large group structures.

Yet these talk structures are very important because they give children many opportunities to use language throughout the school day. These opportunities are simply not available to children whose only audience is the teacher or if they must wait for a turn to speak to the teacher or to the whole class.

Perhaps it's worth restating that oral language, in itself, is not a separate subject to be scheduled into the daily or weekly timetable. Rather, it's a way to learn that cuts across all content areas. For the teacher, then, including opportunities to use oral language becomes a matter of structuring the curriculum to encompass a number of talk structures.

For example, when completing the leaf-collecting activity, the children might have engaged in the initial teacher-directed discussion, written their lists, categorized their own leaves and pasted them on a sheet of paper. Had the activity been carried out like this, much of the valuable talk and, I believe, much of the learning would have been lost.

This is not what happened, however. The activity was, in fact, designed to include a number of talk structures. The children talked to the teacher, to a partner, in small groups, and presented their findings to the class. In the small group activity, particularly, the children were required to make a point clearly and concisely, summarize an idea, or justify an answer. In this way, they not only extended their knowledge of content but were also helped to realize the power of language.

Teacher-to-Large or Small Groups

The time teachers spend talking to students in groups, whether they're small or large, is often regarded as teaching time — a time for imparting information, teaching concepts and focusing thinking by means of questions. Much of this information is imparted by what Carole Edelsky has termed FYIs (For Your Informations). These are short statements made by the teacher to provide information without direct follow-up. For example, during the leaf-collecting activity, the teacher offered the children a great deal of information that he didn't intend to make them directly responsible for remembering. His statements were made simply to provide information. While he naturally hoped that children who were ready would take in and use the information in their own discussions of leaves, he didn't require them to do so.

Many of his FYIs were designed to lay the groundwork for developing concepts and expanding vocabulary. I define concept as the understanding of an idea and vocabulary as the word or words that express that concept. The teacher purposely focused the discussion to highlight both concepts and the matching vocabulary. He introduced vocabulary such as "maroon," "chartreuse," "vein" and "translucent" in a context that was meaningful to the children.

When the teacher held up the maroon leaf and asked the children to do the same, it gave them an opportunity to "see" what maroon means. How different this is from asking children to look up the word in the dictionary!

In his book, *Audio-Visual Methods in Teaching*, Edgar Dale states that the best way to teach a concept is to provide children with a direct, purposeful experience. The least helpful way, on the other hand, is simply to talk about it. If the teacher had used the word, maroon, without displaying anything that color, the effect would have been far less memorable.

The diagram on the following page, borrowed from Dale's book, illustrates the progression of experience from the concrete at the bottom of the cone to the abstract at the top.

Dale suggests that we provide experiences as close to the bottom of the triangle as we can. While this suggestion applies to all students, it is especially important for young learners. We can't always provide hands-on — direct or contrived — experiences, but we do need to move as close to the bottom of the cone as possible, being careful to supply the associated vocabulary. Perhaps we can't, for example, take a field trip, but maybe we can supply an object or a picture.

A Cone of Experience

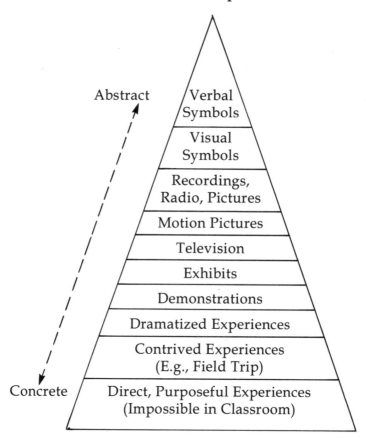

Besides supplying several concrete FYIs aimed at expanding vocabulary and developing concepts, the teacher who designed the leaf-collecting activity used questions to focus and stimulate the children's thinking. In considering the questions he asked, it may be useful to examine both his questioning techniques and the taxonomy of the questions he used to focus thinking.

First, however, let's look at why teachers' questions are important.

- Questions help motivate students by keeping the discussion moving.
- Questions encourage students to contribute new ideas, thus motivating them to search and refine their own understanding.
- They encourage students to clarify their own understandings.
- They provide teachers with valuable feedback about the students' understanding.

For questions to provide the maximum benefit in the classroom, teachers must develop a few simple questioning techniques. The teacher who conducted the leaf-collecting activity used many sound techniques. Perhaps you noticed that he often asked a question, then paused before calling on a child to answer. This technique increased the likelihood that all the students would think about the question because they didn't know who would be called upon to answer. If the teacher had mentioned a child's name before asking the question, the other children might not have listened as carefully.

The pause of three to five seconds before calling a child's name is also important because it provides students with time to think. Research indicates that this pause, which can sometimes seem like a lifetime, is well worth it.

- Students' responses are likely to be longer.
- They are less likely to fail to respond.
- Slower students contribute more.
- Speculative or creative thinking increases.
- Students' confidence increases.

Another useful technique is to engage as many students as possible in responding to the questions. This ensures that their motivation to listen will be high. One way to do this is to ask a question and indicate that students are to signal an answer in some way. In the leaf-collecting activity, for example, the teacher asked all the children who had a leaf of a particular color to hold it up. This way, many, if not all, the children were able to respond to the question.

Another way to encourage multiple responses is to provide students with small slates on which they can write an answer and hold it up. Sometimes, it works better to provide students with small cards that include short responses such as yes and no. As the teacher asks questions, each student can hold up the appropriate card.

Redirection is another technique that encourages high levels of interaction. The teacher asks a question that doesn't have a single answer, then calls upon a number of students to answer in succession. Here's an example:

Teacher: Who do you think was the most courageous character in the book? (Pause) Tom?

Tom: I think it was Jesse.

Teacher: Why, Tom?

Tom: Because he had to work so hard every day.

Teacher: Ann, what do you think?

Ann: I think it was Jesse's father because he had to support the whole family.

T: Joe, what do you think?

The teacher who conducted the leaf-collecting activity used redirection when he asked the children why the leaves had turned brown. This technique encourages students to pay attention and keeps the discussion moving.

Finally, it's also a good idea to encourage the students themselves to ask questions. When they do so, we have an opportunity to model the listening process as we listen carefully to their questions and attempt to respond. We shouldn't be afraid to admit that we don't know all the answers. These occasions provide excellent opportunities for teaching research and library skills as we say, "I honestly don't know. How could we find out?"

When students ask questions, they become more deeply involved in the discussion. Rather than proceeding in one direction from teacher to student, the interaction becomes a two-way scenario. There is also evidence to suggest that the more questions students ask during a discussion, the greater the likelihood that their questions will reflect a higher level of thinking.

Before discussing questions that focus on levels of thinking, let's reflect on students' questions in general and the kinds of questions we hope they will ask. There is a difference between the questions, "May I sharpen my pencil?" and "What are those lines down the center of the leaf?" The first is asked to obtain permission; the second because the student genuinely wants to know something. The first may be absolutely necessary to ensure that the classroom runs smoothly, but it is questions like the second that we really hope to encourage because these are connected to learning.

In her book, *Children's Language and Learning*, Judith Lindfors calls these "curiosity questions." Lindfors and a group of graduate students surveyed classrooms from the preschool level to grade six and categorized the types of questions asked by students. Three categories emerged:

— Curiosity questions: Questions asked to satisfy a desire to know (e.g., Why do snakes shed their skin?).
— Procedural questions: Questions asked to obtain information needed to carry out a procedure in a way considered acceptable to someone else (e.g., Do I have to skip every other line on the page?).
— Social interaction questions: Questions asked to initiate, maintain or clarify a relationship (e.g., Do you want to be in our group?).

Although the study was small, the results were thought-provoking. Lindfors found that in preschool and kindergarten, 45 per cent of 159 questions were social, 33 per cent were curiosity, and 23 per cent procedural. In the primary grades, 14 per cent of 253 questions were social, 19 per cent curiosity, and 66 per cent procedural. In grades four to six, 16 per cent of 116 questions were social, 16 per cent curiosity, and 68 per cent procedural.

It is unfortunate to see that the percentage of curiosity questions shrinks as students progress through the grades. It is precisely these questions that we hope to encourage. Perhaps we can do this by creating interesting experiences, modeling curiosity questions, and allowing students time both to think and to ask questions.

TAXONOMY OF QUESTIONS

Curiosity questions can express — and elicit responses that reflect — many different levels of thought. For example, asking "What color is this leaf?" is qualitatively different from asking "Why do leaves turn brown and fall from the tree?"

Because we hope to encourage students to think about ideas on many different levels, I'll turn now to a discussion of the taxonomy of questions.

A taxonomy is, of course, a classification system. While we need not become unduly preoccupied with defining the exact categories into which questions fall, it is useful to examine a specific taxonomy to help us recognize the kinds of questions we're asking and to focus our own thinking. Various taxonomies have been devised, but the one developed by Benjamin Bloom is probably the best-known and most widely used.

Bloom's Taxonomy

Level 1 — Knowledge

Requires students to recall information exactly as it was learned (e.g., What is the capital of British Columbia?) Questions at this level often start with the words, "who," "what," "where" or "when."

Level 2 — Comprehension

Requires students to go beyond simple recall and demonstrate a grasp of the information by rephrasing material or explaining it in their own words (e.g., What does it mean when we say, "To the victor go the spoils?"). Questions at this level often ask students to describe, compare, contrast, rephrase or explain an idea.

Level 3 — Application

Requires students to apply previously learned material in order to arrive at an answer to a problem (e.g., What's an example of the rule we've been talking about?). Questions at this level often ask students to apply, classify, use, choose, write an example of or solve.

Level 4 — Analysis

Requires students to identify causes, reach conclusions or find supporting evidence (e.g., Why do you think Emily Dickinson was a more effective poet than Robert Frost?). Questions at this level often ask students to identify motives or causes, draw conclusions, determine evidence, support or analyze.

Level 5 — Synthesis

Requires students to think creatively (e.g., What's a good title for this study? Why?). Students are often asked to produce original communications, make predictions or solve problems. Unlike the application level, which requires students to apply facts, problem-solving at this level requires them to come up with original solutions.

Level 6 — Evaluation

Requires students to judge the merit an idea, solution or esthetic work (e.g., Should schools be able to censor library books available to elementary students?). Students are often asked to assess, judge or argue.

While I don't believe we should become slaves to a taxonomy such as Bloom's (in fact, I often have trouble deciding whether a question is at the synthesis or analysis level), I do think that taxonomies provide useful ways of categorizing various questions. We need to be conscious of the kinds of questions we're asking. For example, if we ask only questions at levels one and two, we are not encouraging students to stretch their thinking and may leave the impression that school requires only the restatement of facts.

At the same time, it's important to acknowledge that not all discussions will include questions at all levels. Much will depend on the teacher's objective for a particular discussion. However, over the course of several discussions or lessons on a variety of topics, it is worth reviewing whether we have included questions at all levels.

When working with small groups, it's possible for the teacher to have what could be termed a conversation with students rather than relying so heavily on questions. In these groups, teachers can interact in less formal ways while focusing thinking with both remarks and questions. This often happens when the teacher simply sits in on a small group as a participant or facilitator rather than the designated leader. Acting as another group member, the teacher makes statements, offers opinions, and sometimes asks questions. Here, too, knowledge of a taxonomy can be useful for focusing thinking.

Most instances of this talk structure occur between an individual student and the classroom teacher. During the leaf-collecting activity, for example, the teacher circulated while the children were at their desks recording information. As he did so, he continued to provide FYIs to individual children, asked questions, fielded children's questions and provided needed direction.

Individual conferences often involve teachers with individual students in a more formal setting. Whether they're scheduled or unscheduled, conferences usually involve more detailed and purposeful discussions of students' work than is possible when the teacher is simply circulating around the class. They are typically held to assess a student's writing, reading or mathematics work.

During conferences, it's a good idea to offer students opportunities to take the lead in the discussions. In *Writing: Teachers and Children at Work*, for example, Donald Graves suggests that control of a piece of writing be left in the student's hands. While the teacher may, for example, ask questions, the decision to change a piece remains the student's.

While there are naturally times during conferences when the teacher will ask direct questions or point out strategies or techniques, the atmosphere is more like that of a helpful conversation than a teach-and-test time when the teacher does all the talking and the student all the listening.

Although suitable opportunities are often difficult to find, it's a good idea to make a real effort to find moments for simply chatting with students. This may happen on the playground at recess, at lunchtime or before school. These interactions give children a chance to talk to an adult in an informal setting about topics that may be far removed from the work of the classroom. They also give children opportunities to see teachers outside their classroom roles and provide teachers with opportunities to learn things about the children that may not be possible in the classroom context.

Children also need opportunities to talk to adults other than the teacher. Suggesting that children interview the principal, nurse, custodian, secretary or other school personnel, perhaps during a study unit titled Our School, is one way of initiating this kind of interaction. Questions can be composed ahead of time, the interviewer can receive feedback about the questions from the teacher and the rest of the class, the interview can be conducted, and the interviewer can then report back to the class. As part of a unit called Our Community, students may interview, either in person or by telephone, a variety of people who contribute to the life of the community — shopkeepers, businesspeople, volunteer workers and so on.

To help complete assignments, students often need to obtain specific information. It may be helpful if they realize that libraries are not always the only source of this information. Sometimes it can be obtained by talking to people. For example, during a unit on the judicial system, one grade seven student made arrangements to visit a small claims court and speak to various court officers. Or, in preparation for a class party, students may need to telephone various businesses to check on the price and availability of certain foods or decorations.

The students themselves can also serve as information sources. An open house or school fair, for example, can feature student tour guides whose job it is to explain what has been happening at the school or in the classroom. All the invitations to this event don't necessarily need to be written. If they practice beforehand, students can deliver some of them orally. This also applies to acknowledgments of thanks. When opportunities such as these arise, teachers need to encourage and promote this type of interaction.

Child-to-Child

For the most part, this kind of talk structure occurs informally as children consult each other while they're working. Many teachers demand that students sit quietly and do their own work, but if we are genuinely interested in helping students learn, we must acknowledge that they can — and do — learn from each other.

I recommend that students be free to consult with others during work periods as long as the noise level doesn't rise so high that it interferes with concentration. Students must use their conversation-level voices and there must be areas in the classroom where individual students who don't wish to be disturbed can work independently and quietly.

When they interact with their peers, shy or non-verbal children, as well as children for whom English is a second language, will often use oral language in a way they wouldn't with the teacher or in a group setting. For example, during the journal-writing period in an ungraded primary classroom that I visited weekly, children were encouraged to ask a neighbor for help before going to the teacher. I noticed that two ESL children, Catherine and Hester, sat side by side. While Hester was very shy about using English with the teacher or in a group, she whispered to Catherine and often asked her for help.

The child-to-child talk structure may include children buddy reading with a partner, talking to a partner about a book, a piece of writing or an experience, asking questions, and asking for help in some other way. Many of the interactions last only a few seconds and may include many different individuals over a period of time. When this talk structure works effectively, the teacher is not the sole facilitator of knowledge in the classroom. The students themselves also assume this role.

Sometimes partners are assigned by the teacher or chosen by students for a specific purpose. When this happens, the child-to-child talk structure becomes more formal. During the leaf-collecting activity, for example, children were invited to provide a partner with as much information as possible about their leaves. The teacher structured the activity to accomplish a specific purpose within a finite time period. If this more formal interaction is to work successfully, the teacher must be sensitive to which students work well together.

If students choose their own partners, provision needs to be made for changing pairs who don't work well together. The teacher can do this by stating matter-of-factly, "You didn't work well as partners yesterday. You weren't able to accomplish your task. I'll assign each of you a different partner today and we may try you together again next week." To help a child who is socially isolated and unlikely to be chosen as a partner by other students, the teacher might say, "I would like Michael and Jason to work together. I think this combination will work out well."

When teachers assign the partners, we must be sensitive to the social patterns and conditions within the classroom. For example, girls and boys often prefer to work with a partner of the same sex. These preferences should be honored. Or, some students who are particularly dominant or verbal may completely overshadow a quieter partner. For the most part, these partnerships should be avoided.

Partners work well in a number of classroom situations:

— Drilling each other on math facts, spelling words, etc.
— Checking each other's work — e.g., homework, writing drafts, etc.
— When two heads are better than one.

A partner also works well as an audience for oral language. When students talk to a partner, they have more opportunities to speak than in small or large groups. During the leaf-collecting activity, children were invited to share their information orally with a partner in order to maximize their opportunities to talk and, through this talk, organize their thinking and remember facts and ideas.

It's worth noting that partners need not always be chosen among students in the same classroom. Cross-age partnerships — pairing an older child, perhaps from grade six, with a younger child, perhaps from grade two — are often formed in elementary schools.

These partnerships benefit both parties. The younger child is usually thrilled to receive the personal attention of an older student and can be given much-needed help in learning to read and write. The older student also forms bonds with the younger child and, because the material must be learned before it can be taught to the partner, his or her own academic performance often benefits. This is especially helpful for older children who are behind their classmates academically. For example, few older children would choose to read a primary book for fear of being ridiculed. However, if they must practice reading the book so they can read it aloud to a younger partner, this suddenly becomes an appropriate thing to do.

A specific time is often set aside each week for cross-age partners to work together. For example, a grade five class may get together for 30 minutes a week to read to their partners in grade one. These partnerships may last for a semester or an entire year. The grade five child chooses the book, reads it aloud at least once at home to practice, then reads and talks about it with the younger partner.

A number of experiences might evolve from these once-a-week sessions. For example, the partners may complete units of study or go on field trips together. In one school, cross-age partners visit a pumpkin patch early every October. Each pair is responsible for locating a pumpkin, which is brought back to the classroom and carved into a jack-o'-lantern. Before carving the pumpkin, the partners work out a design together, a task that involves much planning and use of oral language. A contest is held and winners are selected in many categories — the funniest, scariest, smallest, largest and so on. Photographs of the event are placed in a class book so that children can use this record as a springboard for further talk. The pair then brainstorm Halloween words and write stories and poems to share with the combined classes. In all the activities, younger and older children are equal participants.

In other schools, cross-age partnerships are extended to cross-age teams. Children at various age levels form a team and get together several times during the year to work cooperatively on a project. One school, for example, decided on a Halloween theme and organized activities like measuring and weighing pumpkins at a math center. For six consecutive Thursday afternoons, a team of two children from grade one, two from grade two and two from grade three worked together at the various centers. The objective was for the children to encourage each other as they worked together to achieve a common goal. Teachers talked about encouragement, what it looks like and what it sounds like when children encourage each other. While the products produced at each center were evaluated, so was the amount of encouragement displayed by each team.

Child-to-Small Group

An effective pattern for introducing small-group work is to begin with a teacher-directed large group experience, then invite small groups either to discuss the experience or to provide a product related to the experience. The small groups then report back to the large group. This pattern can be illustrated as follows:

Large Group → Small Group → Large Group

The pattern can be used over and over in a variety of contexts and subject areas, such as social studies projects, science experiments, language arts and reading assignments, making up original games in physical education and so on. The teacher-directed large group provides direction, motivation and clarification, the small groups provide an opportunity for maximum participation, and reporting back to the large group builds in accountability for the small groups and provides an audience for their work.

A lesson based on John Bianchi's *The Swine Snafu* provides a good example of how this pattern can work. The story is about a family of pigs and a family of boars who live next door to each other. Mrs. Pig is neat, precise and methodical, while Mrs. Boar is fun-loving, easy-going and disorganized. Both Mrs. Pig and Mrs. Boar give birth to babies in the same hospital on the same day. As the story progresses, we see that the Pigs have children with Mrs. Boar's personality and vice versa. The Boars love to play baseball and are always hitting their balls into the Pigs' prized gladioli. The Pigs look down on the Boars and call the police whenever the Boars' baseball lands in their yard. Is it possible that there was a mix-up at the hospital?

The story can be interpreted on many different levels. It is about pigs and boars, about getting along with neighbors, about recognizing and valuing differences, about accepting children unconditionally, about world peace. The interpretation is up to the reader.

Begin by showing the cover of the book to the class and inviting the children to predict what the story might be about. List their predictions on the chalkboard. You may even provide a hint like, "In this story, the Pigs and the Boars don't get along. What do you think might cause this problem?"

After their ideas have been discussed, read the book aloud to the class or, if there are enough copies, invite the children to read it silently on their own. Afterwards, discuss briefly what the story is about. If the children's ideas don't go beyond suggesting that it's about pigs and boars playing baseball, you may need to prompt them by saying something like, "Well, I think it might be about how to raise children."

Then, organize the children into small groups and invite them to discuss the book and reach a consensus about the topic of the story. Ask them to represent their ideas using crayons and a large piece of art paper. Each group must do only one drawing and all members must contribute. The drawing need not be realistic and the ideas can be represented using only symbols or colors. Once the picture is complete, each small group presents its picture to the large group and fields questions.

Successful small-group work doesn't just happen. It must be carefully planned. If we simply instruct students to divide into small groups and complete an assignment, the experience may be disastrous, leaving us wary of trying this talk structure again. We may even blame it on the students, saying things like, "My class this year is so noisy that group work isn't profitable."

Before giving up, however, it's worth reviewing our organization and remembering that students need time to learn group interaction skills. When organizing small group work, teachers need to structure situations that require productive talk and help students function successfully in small-group discussion situations.

We can do a number of things to ensure that talk is productive.

Offer students responsibility for creating a common product.

A product is something students are to produce as a result of participating in the group. This might be a summary, list, picture, game, discussion or short dramatization. The key is that the group must plan together, execute the plan together, and produce only one product. If each student produces an individual product, then the talk needed to plan and execute the plan together becomes unnecessary. In the sample lesson on *The Swine Snafu*, if each student had been asked to draw an individual picture to represent the story, then no discussion of the meaning of the book would have been necessary. The talk involved in the process of drawing — e.g., "Put the grass lower down on the page," and "Do you think we should have the baseball diamond here?" — would also have been unnecessary. By assigning a common product, however, we almost guarantee that this kind of talk will take place.

Build in student accountability.

This can usually be accomplished by requiring that the product be finished in a given amount of time and shown, demonstrated, or presented to someone. In the case of a discussion, a group secretary can keep notes. This helps ensure that students will organize themselves and remain on task.

When we first introduce small-group work in the classroom, it's often a good idea to ask students to produce — rather than discuss — something. Of course, the two can be combined as in the sample lesson on *The Swine Snafu*. The goal of creating a concrete product, such as a drawing, rather than simply talking takes the focus off language skills until the students become more experienced. The actual making of the product will elicit productive talk.

Emphasize the process.

Although the students' goal is to create a product, we, as teachers, must think about the process. It is more important for children to struggle with and talk about the meaning of, for example, *The Swine Snafu* and how it can be represented than to produce a beautiful picture. In a grade seven classroom where I tried a similar activity, the group that produced the sketchiest picture had spent so long discussing the meaning of the story that little time was left for drawing.

Help Students Function Successfully

Every teacher knows that plans that look good on paper don't necessarily translate into successful classroom activities. Students may need to be taught interactional skills such as how to form groups, how to talk to one another while in the groups, and how to bring a sense of closure to the group experience. These skills fall into three main categories: forming skills, operating skills, and functioning skills. These categories are condensed from a list of forming, functioning, formulating, and fermenting skills presented by David Johnson, Roger Johnson and Edythe Holubec in their book, *Circles of Learning: Cooperation in the Classroom.*

In the primary grades, it's a good idea to begin with a maximum of three group members and, in the higher grades, no more than five. This ensures that the children, who are working on a single product, will have plenty of opportunity to participate and talk.

Initially, it's probably best for the teacher to make up the groups, although doing this successfully requires considerable sensitivity. Teachers need to notice if there are combinations of students that don't work well together and watch the power structure in groups. Students who don't participate in one group because they feel dominated may participate more readily when placed in another group with students who have less dominant personalities. An atmosphere that encourages children to take risks needs to be fostered in the groups as well as in the classroom.

Depending upon the task, I recommend that group members remain together for a period of several weeks. Keeping groups stable for an extended period gives students time to get to know one another and to establish an atmosphere in which members are willing to take risks. It also allow groups to evaluate the skills they need to work on and make improvements.

Once the groups are established, a number of other forming skills need to be explained and modeled. Through practice and discussion, students need to learn how to move quickly and quietly into their groups, whether this involves moving desks or simply going to specific areas. It may be necessary to walk them through this process many times.

After students have moved into groups, they need to learn to stay with the group rather than move around the room. Specific rules for this need to be established and discussed. Further, students need to practice using conversation-level voices so that the noise level in the room is conducive to learning. Social skills such as using someone's name, looking at a speaker, and keeping hands and feet to oneself are all forming skills.

OPERATING SKILLS

Operating skills include basic practices such as requesting clarification or help if the assignment is not clear, keeping on task or topic, listening while others are speaking, and participating by stating one's ideas or asking questions. Again, we can't expect students to use these skills intuitively. Rather, they must be taught, using techniques such as discussion, modeling and demonstration.

FUNCTIONING SKILLS

Functioning skills include more advanced practices such as expressing ideas clearly and supporting them with reasons, summarizing, if necessary, before the group moves on, asking for justification of another's idea without criticizing, extending another's idea by providing additional information, and integrating several ideas into a plan. These skills, too, need to be explained, practiced and evaluated.

TEACHING GROUP-WORK SKILLS

Forming, operating and functioning skills are developmental in nature. It stands to reason, for example, that a group that can't successfully practice many of the forming skills will run into difficulty with the functioning skills. By the same token, if a group can't stay on task, it will be hard for individual members to support ideas with reasons.

Because of this, it's advisable to start by practicing the forming skills. On the day of the first small-group session, the teacher can brainstorm with the class to make a list of things students will need to do to form groups. If the students don't suggest the forming skills mentioned previously, the teacher may raise them. Once they've been discussed, the skills can then be transferred to a wall chart for review before subsequent small-group sessions.

To begin, the teacher might pick one skill, such as moving into groups, to demonstrate and walk through with students. Then students can try it on their own with the teacher monitoring. After students have moved into groups, they can work with the teacher to evaluate what happened and how to improve next time. Several practice sessions may be required before the teacher can say, "Move into your discussion groups," and expect students to do it quickly and quietly. While this may seem like a time-consuming process to go through with each skill, it will pay dividends in time saved throughout the school year.

After the discussion activity, it's important for the groups to evaluate themselves. In the primary grades, the teacher might chart a series of short statements such as, "We all shared today," "We used names," and "We liked being in the group today." If a happy and sad face follow each statement, the teacher can read the statements aloud one at a time while the students circle one of the two faces.

Here's an example of an evaluation form that might be used by groups in the higher grades:

Oral Language Group Report

Names _____

Date _____

What was the group's task or focus?

What was the best thing about the way you worked together?

What did you do specifically to accomplish the task?

Think of one problem you had.
    What was it?
    Why do you think it happened?
    How did the group solve it?
    What else could you have done?
    Would you use the same solution again?
    What specific plans do you have for improvement?

One person can be appointed to read the questions aloud, lead a discussion and fill in the blanks. If there are more than five students in the group, both a secretary and a leader may be appointed. The first couple of times groups evaluate themselves, the teacher might read through the form with the whole class and elicit individual answers before suggesting that the groups fill in their own forms.

If the completed forms are collected and stored in a group folder, they can be used as the basis for instruction before the next small-group session. For example, if three of five groups list the participation of some members as a problem, the teacher might choose this as the focus of a five-minute mini-lesson like this:

Teacher: I looked over your evaluation forms and, in some groups, it seems that everyone is not participating. Let's brainstorm to come up with some things we could do if that happens again.

Students suggest a number of ideas such as take turns, make everyone say something, appoint a leader who calls on everybody, and everyone has to say something before anyone gets a second turn.

Teacher: Do you think everyone must have a turn?

Students: Yes!

Teacher: What if someone is shy or just hasn't had enough time to feel comfortable?

Student: Well, no. They wouldn't have to then.

Teacher: What if we did something like this? When you get into your groups today, appoint one person to make sure everyone has a chance to participate. If they see that someone hasn't had much of an opportunity, they could say something like, "Susie, do you have anything that you want to add or any questions?" This would give Susie a chance to speak, but she would still feel free to say no. Let's try it for today and see how it works.

Once students have mastered the forming skills, we can move on to the operating skills. Again, we can brainstorm to come up with a list of skills needed to keep groups running smoothly. The teacher can contribute skills the students didn't mention and these can be incorporated onto a wall chart for future reference. A typical mini-lesson on one of these skills might look like this:

Teacher: I looked over your evaluation forms from the last group session and noticed that some groups were having trouble staying on task. Some people seemed to be playing with things in their desks rather than working on the booklets. Let's think of some things we could do if this happens again.

Students make several suggestions as the teacher writes them down. These include: tell the teacher; remind the group of the time limit; tell the troublemaker to be quiet; and say, "Get to work."

Teacher: I think that these are good ideas. You seem to be saying that the group may need reminding. That might be hard to do without looking like a tattletale. Suppose we were to appoint one person in the group to have the official job of reminding the group. This way, there would be nothing personal. It would just be that person's job. As soon as you move into your groups today, how about appointing one person to say, "We're off topic," every time it happens? Would you be willing to try it and we'll evaluate how it works?

Students: Yes.

Teacher: Fine, then let's move into groups.

Every time the group meets, the first task is always to hand out the group folder and examine the last question on the evaluation form indicating specific plans for improvement. This reminds the group of what they intend to work on during the session. As mentioned previously, one advantage of keeping group membership stable for a period of weeks is to encourage continuity in this group evaluation process.

Once the groups have mastered the forming and the operating skills, the teacher can use the same process to focus on the functioning skills. A typical mini-lesson might look like this:

Teacher: Last time you met in groups, I was circulating around the room and listening to what many people were saying. It's very important to be able to disagree with someone without making them feel wrong. This could be called stating your own ideas without criticizing someone else. Let's play a little game. I'll say something critical and you suggest another way of saying the same thing by suggesting an idea. For example, if I say, "That's dumb," you might say, "I think we should do it this way." If I say, "That color is ugly," what could you say instead?

Student: Let's use the green.

Teacher: Okay. How about if I said, "You're wrong. Jesse's father is the character." What could you say instead?

Student: I think Jesse's father is the main character.

Teacher: As we're working today, let's keep this in mind and try to state our own ideas without criticizing others.

Whenever possible, mini-lessons are based on the students' needs, as indicated by the teacher's observations and the students' group evaluation form. Because of this, the lessons may not progress in an orderly fashion through the forming, operating and functioning skills. However, these skills and the skills listed on the wall chart at the beginning of the school year can serve as a basis both for mini-lessons and instruction. It is not unusual to find that some skills need to be the focus of repeated mini-lessons while others need not be presented at all because students have them well under control.

Once groups get into the routine of evaluating themselves, forms for individual evaluation can be introduced. These help individuals think through their contributions to the group and make plans for improvement. Here's an example:

Oral Language Report on Myself

Name _____

Date _____

I was talking to _____

We were doing _____

My last improvement plan was to _____

	Yes	No	Sometimes
I shared my ideas.	___	___	___
I listened to others.	___	___	___
I spoke loudly/softly enough.	___	___	___
I answered others' questions.	___	___	___
I remained on task/topic.	___	___	___
I encouraged others to participate.	___	___	___
I presented my ideas clearly.	___	___	___
I disagreed without hurting others' feelings.	___	___	___
I summarized or repeated my ideas if necessary.	___	___	___
I gave reasons for my opinions.	___	___	___

My next plan for improvement is to _____

If the forms are kept in individual folders, the students' plans for improvement noted at the bottom can be reviewed before starting the next small-group session. A few times during the year, especially before issuing progress reports, teachers may invite individuals and groups to fill out summary evaluation forms like the following:

Individual Evaluation Form

Name _____

Date _____

The most important things I learned about myself in group situations were:

The activity could have been more beneficial to me if:

_____

Group Evaluation Form

Group No. _____

Group Members _____

List the initial strengths of the group.

What were your most important problems? Why did they develop? How did you solve — or attempt to solve — them? What improvements were made?

What was the greatest benefit of group work over individual work?

Would you want to use groups again as a basis for learning content? Why?

Time and patience are the keys to helping children reach the point where they can work effectively in groups. We can't expect students to be completely successful the first — or even the second or third — time we try it. We must begin by slowly building the necessary skills and evaluating the students' success over time, moving forward only as we feel comfortable. Perhaps in the beginning, we could try small-group work twice a week or during one or two selected units through the school year.

Cooperative learning is a specialized form of small-group interaction in which children work together in small, heterogeneous groups with the ultimate goal of producing individual learning.

Because cooperative learning groups require students to accomplish a mutual goal, they are, in this sense, indistinguishable from other small groups. However, they differ from other small groups in several important ways. They're structured to promote positive interdependence. Students are in a situation together, and must realize that they will succeed or fail together. This realization can be fostered several ways:

— Mutual goals: Students perceive that individual goals are the same as group goals.
— Division of labour: The project is outlined and each student is given a specific task that will ultimately contribute to an integrated whole. For example, each student might be responsible for researching a different aspect of a particular industry.
— Division of resources or information: These may be divided up in much the same way as the labor.
— Assigning specific roles: This, too, is similar to the division of labor. In preparing a written report, one person may do the writing, one the typing, one the art work and so on.
— Giving joint rewards: These rewards usually take the form of grades. All the group members share the same grade, though the teacher may wish to build in the potential for some variations.

Because each member of a cooperative learning group is responsible for mastering all the material and each must be able to explain or perhaps take a test on it, the level of individual accountability is high. If students were completing a study of a particular industry, for example, each group member might be responsible for researching one aspect. However, each student would also be responsible for knowing about all aspects of the project. Group members are often required to teach their part of a group project to others.

Cooperative learning also requires students to learn and use interpersonal and social skills. These are similar to the forming, operating and functioning skills discussed earlier. The goal of cooperative learning is not only to master specific content, but also to master the skills required to interact and collaborate with others.

The teacher's role is to specify both the academic and cooperative goals, to make decisions about placing students in groups, to be clear about the assignment and explain procedures, and to monitor the group's effectiveness in achieving both the academic and cooperative goals. Academic goals don't usually differ from objectives teachers have always written. In *Circles of Learning: Cooperation in the Classroom*, however, the authors spell out several cooperative goals:

Forming Groups	*Managing Groups*
Moving into	Sharing ideas
Using quiet voices	Reporting ideas
Listening to others	Watching time
Taking turns	Asking for help
Staying on task	Paraphrasing ideas
Finishing task	Saying how you feel
Recording ideas	Being enthusiastic
Following directions	Praising others
Using names	Helping others
Encouraging others	Expressing support

Maximizing Learning	**Stimulating Thinking**
Asking probing questions	Criticizing ideas, not people
Checking for agreement	Appreciating others' viewpoints
Directing group's work	
Elaborating	Achieving consensus
Summarizing ideas	Integrating ideas
Checking for accuracy	Checking for validity
Relieving tension	Asking for justification
Showing acceptance of others	Giving reasons
	Defending viewpoint

In cooperative learning groups, these skills are often stressed by assigning roles. For example, one person may be assigned the role of praiser. Throughout the group session, it is this person's responsibility to look for opportunities to praise others. Someone else may be assigned the role of checker. It is this person's responsibility to clarify anything that is not clear by making inquiries such as, "Did you say that...?"

Cooperative Learning by Robert Slavin and *Leading the Cooperative School* by David and Roger Johnson are good sources of a more detailed discussion on cooperative learning.

Child-to-Large Group

Through this classroom interaction pattern, children gain experience in making more formal types of presentations. It's similar to public speaking in many ways. Children must learn to project their voices and vary their tonal qualities, maintain eye contact with a large number of people, and be aware of their posture and facial expressions. These skills do not come naturally. They must be demonstrated, modeled and practiced.

It's a good idea to introduce this kind of interaction in relatively non-threatening situations. For example, a small group might be invited to present its work to the large group. This not only makes the small group accountable for its work, but also gives members an opportunity to stand in front of the large group with the support of peers. Children who are shy or for whom English is a problem can be given a role that involves little language, such as holding up a picture while others explain it and answer questions. Little by little, as they begin to feel more comfortable, these children can assume larger roles. These presentations are usually not rehearsed extensively ahead of time. Rather, group members simply tell about, demonstrate or show their work in an informal setting.

Encouraging students to become experts in something also provides them with opportunities to speak in front of a large group. In the primary grades, this can be done through show-and-tell and, in the intermediate grades, through activities such as following a news story that is of particular interest. Students can gather information from TV, radio, newspapers or magazines and report the latest developments to the class each morning.

Teachers can also promote this interaction pattern by appointing a teacher of the day. This "teacher" may be responsible for duties such as calling the roll, discussing the weather chart, leading show-and-tell, or making announcements. For the first few weeks, the teacher will need to model leading these activities. By late October or early November, however, even children in grade one are able to take over many of these duties.

Other large group presentations, such as book talks, oral reports, or formal demonstrations, may be prepared ahead of time by students.

Book talks not only give students opportunities to speak in front of a large group but also create interest in literature. The idea is to present the book by announcing the title and perhaps showing the cover, then tell just enough about it to interest others in reading it. A short passage may also be read aloud to build interest or illustrate an author's writing style. Ideally, the book should be available to students in either the classroom or the school library.

Book talks should be limited to three or four minutes and no more than two or three books should be presented in one day. At the beginning of the school year, the teacher models how to give book talks by sharing personal favorites. After the teacher has presented several books, the students can take over this responsibility.

Book talks can be organized in a variety of ways. If there is a period for silent reading, two students each day may volunteer to present a book during the last few minutes of the period or books can be presented daily as part of the morning routine. The talks should be kept short and snappy, leaving students wanting more rather than bored.

As students are offered more choice and work in the classroom diversifies, there are many opportunities for making presentations and conducting demonstrations. In addition to book talks, these can take the form of oral reports where one group, for example, studies the customs of a particular country while another studies means of transportation and communication. This information needs to be shared, not merely to encourage children to give oral reports, but primarily to inform other groups. This provides an authentic reason for presenting the report. The group presenting the report plans the information that will be included and decides how to make it interesting. In some cases, the teacher may stipulate that the audience will write about or discuss what they learned from the report. This introduces an element of accountability that helps students view listening to an oral report as a way to learn.

Besides reports, students can also share role drama, puppet presentations or readers' theater presentations. They may be asked to teach a song or a game to the group or introduce or thank a speaker. Many opportunities to engage in large-group interactions are created throughout the school year.

Planning Your Own Talk Structures

When planning classroom activities, there are lots of things to think about. What activities are likely to work well with individuals, partners, small groups or large groups? How might you provide FYIs or use questions both to provide and elicit ideas? As you work to organize activities into various talk structures, I hope you'll come to feel comfortable restructuring common classroom experiences to provide for a maximum of productive oral language — both talk and listening.

Whenever possible, the students' own interests should provide a springboard to classroom activities. In one grade one class, for example, the children had read several of Bill Peet's books during their silent-reading and buddy-reading times. These books, which they had selected themselves, turned out to be favorites. Because of this interest, the teacher and children decided to make a bulletin board illustrating Peet's works. This involved many discussions as well as art and writing activities. The children also formed small groups to talk about books and individuals presented books to the class during the last five minutes of silent-reading time.

Marcia Brown's book, *Stone Soup*, is an old favorite that children love. It's about a peddlar who arrives in a very poor town and claims that he can make soup from a stone. When the townspeople don't believe him, the peddlar asks for a large pot of water and, when it is boiling, drops in a stone. After stirring the water he exclaims, "Delicious, truly delicious! The only thing that would make it better is a bit of carrot."

One of the townspeople rushes home and comes back with some carrots. The peddlar adds the carrots to the soup, tastes it and exclaims, "Delicious, truly delicious! The only thing that would make it better is a bit of onion."

Somebody else supplies the onion. This continues until all sorts of vegetables, meat, and salt and pepper have been added. The townspeople are so amazed that the peddlar could make delicious soup from a stone that they invite him to become a permanent resident.

All sorts of activities could follow the reading of this book. Although we don't share a common classroom experience, I'll provide some examples. However, you know the children in your classroom best and only you can select the activities that will match their needs, interests and abilities.

— Invite students to retell the story using a flannelboard with cut-outs of various vegetables.
— Brings various vegetables, including some unusual ones, to class. Invite children to examine and discuss them.
— Sort and classify vegetables in various ways.
— Examine recipes for vegetable soup and choose, or invent, a class recipe.
— Make stone soup. Encourage children to cut up the vegetables and make the soup.
— Invite parents or another class for soup and crackers.
— Make vegetable prints at the art center.
— Grow some vegetables in the classroom. Sweet potatoes, onions, carrots and turnips grow well in water. Roots can be started by supporting the vegetable with toothpicks in a transparent container of water. When roots appear, the vegetables can be transferred to soil outside, if a spot exists, or taken home by individual students.

When considering these activities or others, ask how they might be planned to include various talk structures. How might the children work best individually, as partners, or in small or large groups? What information, vocabulary, and concepts might be developed?

The aim of this chapter has been to encourage you to consider both the curriculum — the curriculum set out in guide books and textbooks as well as the curriculum that emanates from the students' interests — and ways to reorganize it to include opportunities for students to participate in various talk structures. The activities based on *Stone Soup* may provide useful practice.

. . . .

FUNCTIONS OF LANGUAGE

When planning for — and assessing — students' use of oral language in the classroom, we must consider another important aspect of the talk structures we create. As students interact, they use language for a variety of purposes — to inform one another about something, to predict what will happen, to maintain social interactions and so on. These purposes — the functions of language — are as vital to maintaining communication as the actual words spoken or the grammatical context of those words. This chapter will examine the functions of language that are integral to many of the classroom activities discussed in the previous chapter. In addition, we'll look at techniques for assessing how students use language.

Sometimes the function of a particular utterance is easy to spot. For example, I might say to a student, "Carol, open the back windows please." This request is clearly made for the purpose of controlling.

Sometimes, however, the language function is not as easy to discern. For example, I might say to you, "It's hot in here." Is this a statement of my physical condition or an indirect request for a glass of water or for someone to open a window? This depends on a variety of factors and, in fact, might be impossible for us to figure out without a more detailed description of the context. Who was present? Were we in a hot stuffy room with the windows closed? Was water available? All this aside, one thing remains certain: if I meant it as a request and you perceived it as a statement, we have not communicated.

Although determining the function of utterances is integral to the communication process, this is an element of language that most of us rarely consider. In my experience, teachers know a great deal about students' vocabulary levels and their ability to use standard grammar and pronunciation, but we rarely think about how students use language. Yet, if students cannot use language appropriately for a broad range of functions and cannot perceive the functions for which others use language, they will have serious communication problems.

Let's look at some classroom situations to examine the language functions that are evident.

First, we're in a kindergarten classroom just before the dismissal bells rings. The children have been told to clean up and gather on the carpet. The teacher says, "I like the way Pamjit has gotten her coat and is sitting quietly." In making this statement, she may be using language for more than one function. While she is certainly praising Pamjit, her primary purpose may be to encourage the other children to get their coats and sit quietly on the carpet, too. However, if the children don't recognize the teacher's statement as a request, perhaps even a directive, they have missed the meaning and communication has not taken place.

Let's move to a grade six classroom where the teacher is forming small groups for a social studies project. He says, "I'd like Alec and Sonia to be in different groups today." In all probability, he is giving an order, not stating a preference. Should the students fail to recognize the statement as an order, the teacher will likely restate it more explicitly by saying, "Alec and Sonia will be in different groups today."

The Five Functions of Language

In school, students must use — and understand language that is used — for a wide range of functions. As illustrated in the preceding examples, one fundamental purpose of using language is to control the behavior of others. This may include making requests, demands, appeals and threats as well as giving commands.

In our book, *Language Functions for School Success*, Robert Shafer, Karen Smith and I reorganized a number of the categories articulated by Joan Tough to present a simplified and workable system for recognizing language functions. The following chart indicates the five overall functions we identified, as well as sub-functions and examples of each.

Functions of Language

Asserting and Maintaining Social Needs

Sub-Functions	Examples
Asserting personal rights and/or needs	I want some juice. Give it to me. It's mine. I'm first 'cause I'm the oldest. I hit him because he hit me first.
Asserting negative expressions: criticizing, arguing, threatening and expressing negative opinions	I need a blue crayon. You're talking too much. I told you to quit it. Stop it or I'll tell. That looks dumb.
Asserting positive expressions	Yes, I think so, too. I like your building. It tastes good to me.
Requesting an opinion	Do you like this?
Incidental expressions	Oh, gee. Good grief!

Controlling

Sub-Functions	Examples
Controlling actions of self and others	Turn it around (to self). Get one egg. Give me the blue one. Put your name at the top and I'll give it to the teacher.
Requesting directions	How do you do this? Where shall I put this?
Requesting others' attention	Watch this. Look here.

Informing

Sub-Functions	Examples
Commenting on past or present events: labeling, noting details, specific incidents and sequence (includes statements made in both first and third persons)	That's a car. It's blue and white. I have some red paint. He put on the red before the yellow.
Comparing	The first bus is longer than the second.
Making generalizations based on specific events and details	My brother is sick today. The cars were in an accident.
Requesting information	What color is this?

Forecasting and Reasoning

Sub-Functions	Examples
Noting or speculating about cause-and-effect relationships	The bridge fell because the logs were too heavy. If you want the bottle to float, you'll have to put on the cap.
Speculating about an event	It might rain tomorrow. That probably won't work.
Noting or speculating about an event followed by a conclusion (includes drawing conclusions)	You're so tall, you'll have to bend over. We better not run away from home. We might get hungry.
Requesting a reason	Why can't I go? Why does this happen?

Projecting

Sub-Functions	Examples
Projecting oneself into feelings and reactions of others	He's feeling sad. He's probably mad about it.
Projecting oneself into experiences of others	I wouldn't like to live in the zoo with tigers.

When we make known our personal needs, desires and preferences, we are using language to assert and maintain our social needs. Children younger than seven are particularly egocentric and tend to view a situation almost exclusively in relation to its effect on their own rights and needs. They often communicate these effects very assertively and may end up criticizing, threatening or arguing. As they grow older, they learn to assert their rights and needs more appropriately, often by negotiating with others and taking turns.

Comments that keep a conversation going are also included in this category. These often take the form of interjections like, "Good grief!" or "You don't mean it!" By using these expressions, we hold up our end of a conversation, show interest and encourage the speaker to continue.

CONTROLLING

Language used to control is straightforward. It's the language we use when we want to get a job done. It may be direct, as in, "Pass me the scissors," or "Let's use the green paint to color the trees." It may also be indirect, as in, "Can you reach the blue paper on the top shelf?" In this instance, the response expected is not, "Yes." Rather, the listener is expected to get the paper. If I say, "Those cookies look delicious," I may be hinting that I'd like to be offered one. Language used to control asks for an action to be completed.

Children older than seven usually use this language to control others. Younger children, however, may use it to control themselves. For example, as a kindergarten child plays with a car at the block center, the teacher may hear her say, "Turn, turn, turn to the right — that's right, now into the garage." For this child, talking aloud to herself is a way of directing her own actions. With older children and adults this language becomes subvocal, although all of us have probably been caught talking to ourselves from time to time.

INFORMING

This function is used when asking for or imparting information. Children often impart information by labeling, recalling specific events, comparing or making general observations.

Many of the questions children ask are requests for information. Throughout the school day, children make statements as well as ask and answer questions in order to inform and be informed. This may occur in the context of a formal lesson when a child says, "The capital of Australia is Canberra." It may also occur in the context of a casual conversation when a child says, "My next-door neighbors moved away."

Because communication involves the ability not only to use language to accomplish a specific purpose but also to understand the function when others are using it, children must be able to recognize teachers' requests for information. We often ask questions to test students' knowledge, not because we genuinely want to know. Some children may not recognize that test or display questions require answers because they reason that the teacher already knows.

FORECASTING AND REASONING

Language used to forecast and reason is the language of curiosity. It is language that seeks to discover, probe, question and speculate. It requests and gives reasons. The question, "Why would we fall off the earth without gravity?" and the answer, "Because the force of gravity pulls objects toward the earth," are examples of language used to forecast and reason.

In *Language in Primary Classrooms*, Connie and Harold Rosen remark on children's natural curiosity and excitement about their world and suggest that school should be a place for this to happen. They say, "All too often this curiosity is not sanctioned in school and (children's) attention is directed instead to barren collections of information which give no hint of the excitement of discovery and doubt. Small wonder then if their language becomes barren too. It is only those affairs which create real preoccupation which can make them reach out for the language to express new understanding, new questions, and new perceptions. This is the language of curiosity. It may express itself as a set of observations or be explicitly speculative, but it is always the result of the child's own probing into the working of the world."

PROJECTING

Language used for this purpose expresses what it would be like if we were someone — or something — else. It often also involves language used for other purposes, such as informing, reasoning or forecasting within the context of being someone or something else. For example, the statement, "If the movie made her feel sad, she should have stayed home," also involves reasoning, while the statement, "He will feel trapped if he goes inside the cave," involves forecasting. In both instances, the statements occur in the context of imagining what someone else would do or say.

Using language to project is often much more difficult for young children than using it for purposes like informing or asserting and maintaining social needs. In order to project, they must extend their imagination to encompass the point of view of another.

Encouraging Use of Language for Different Functions

Within the context of the classroom, students need both to use language and to understand how it is used for these five basic functions. To do this, they need to hear the functions modeled appropriately in a variety of situations and, if necessary, explained. In addition, they need opportunities to practice using language for a variety of purposes and to receive feedback.

For example, when the grade six teacher mentioned earlier said, "I'd like Alec and Sonia to be in different groups today," he was modeling an indirect form of language used to control. If some students didn't understand what he meant, he could have explained that Alec and Sonia were to be in different groups. As children work with these functions within the classroom, their ability to recognize and use them appropriately in a variety of situations increases.

To provide students with opportunities to practice and receive feedback in using and understanding the basic language functions, teachers may create situations that require them to use language for particular purposes. At this stage, it's important to note that a given situation may elicit more than one language function and that a single statement may have more than one language function. If we return to the example of the teacher who said, "I like the way Pamjit has gotten her coat and is sitting quietly," we can see that the primary function is to control. However, in praising Pamjit, the teacher is also using language to assert and maintain social needs.

TEACHERS' QUESTIONS AND DIALOGUE

Although teachers' questions were discussed in the previous chapter, we'll revisit this topic from a slightly different perspective. Dialogue refers to statements that invite responses from students although they are not couched in the form of questions.

Questions and dialogue can be used to elicit not only a particular level of thought, but also specific language functions. For example, after reading a passage from a novel, I might ask, "How do you think the character feels in that situation?" In doing so, I am eliciting language used for projecting. Or, during a science experiment on completing an electrical circuit, I might ask, "Will the light turn on if I touch these two wires and, if so, why?" In this case, I am eliciting language used to forecast and reason.

While it's a good idea for teachers to be aware of the language functions that can be elicited through questions and dialogue, it's worth remembering that these are not a separate subject. Rather, they should be integrated naturally into the curriculum. We don't plan activities and ask questions for the sole purpose of eliciting a particular level of thinking or a particular language function, but as a way of discussing and learning whatever we happen to be studying.

Here are some suggestions for eliciting various language functions through the use of teacher questions and dialogue:

Asserting and Maintaining Social Needs

— Ask for students' opinions. For example, after reading a book aloud to the class, ask questions such as, "Did you like the book?" or "What did you dislike about it?" Or, after attending a performance or going on a field trip ask, "What was your favorite part?"
— Ask students about their needs. For example, rather than anticipating what you think students need, try encouraging them to tell you what their needs are. As a student begins a project, you might ask,"What will you need in the way of materials?" "What help will you need

from me?" "What help will you need from the librarian and other members of the class?"

— Ask for students' suggestions. For example, when establishing classroom rules at the beginning of the year, invite suggestions and list them on the chalkboard, then ask, "Who could agree with this one?" Or, when planning a class party or event, ask, "What will we need to do?" and "Who could agree with that?"

Controlling

— Ask students for directions — make them the experts. For example, ask, "How could I do that math problem to get the same answer you did?" "How do I manage to put that puzzle together?" or "How do I play that game on the computer?"

Informing

— Plan activities that require lists. For example, you might say, "The story we're going to read is about a teddy bear. Let's list everything we know about teddy bears," or "What I have in my hand is a magnet. What do you know about magnets?"

— Plan activities that require students to tell about something. For example, you might say, "Tell me about your new bicycle," or "John has researched the resources of India for us and he's ready to tell the class what he's found out."

— Plan activities that require students to make comparisons. For example, you might say, "We've all had a chance to feel the silk and the burlap. How are they alike? How are they different?" or "How is Sonia's picture like Gurmeet's?"

Forecasting and Reasoning

— Ask "why" questions when the answer is not obvious. For example, during a science experiment on buoyancy, ask, "Why did this bottle sink while this one is still floating?" or, when establishing classroom rules, ask, "Why would it be a good idea to make a rule against chewing gum in the classroom?"

— Ask for predictions. For example, show the cover of a book and ask, "What do you think this book will be about?" Or, stop at predetermined points during the reading to ask, "What do you think will happen next?" and "Do you think this will work?"

Projecting

— Question students while they are playing a role. For example, the students may play the role of a character in a book or a historical figure. As you question them, they are to answer as if they are the character.
— Investigate other viewpoints. Read aloud a book and then ask questions such as, "If you were the younger brother in this story, what would life be like for you?" "If you were the older brother, would it be different?" and "How do you think the little sister is feeling?"

CLASSROOM ACTIVITIES

The activities listed in the previous section cast the teacher in the role of questioner. In these situations, only two talk structures are possible — teacher-to-child or teacher-to-large or small group.

It isn't possible for the teacher to ask questions or engage in dialogue when child-to-child, child-to-small group or child-to-large group talk structures are created. These activities, which may include oral reports, show-and-tell, or carrying out a science experiment in a small group, must be structured so that they elicit language functions in different ways.

The context both elicits and limits appropriate language. We can see this in the following exchange:

A: Give it here, Bob.

B: Here!

C: I'm away.

A: C'mon, John.

B: Great pass!

C: Hand it here.

This dialogue makes no sense at all — unless we know that the speakers are in the middle of a basketball game. The nature of the game both elicits — and limits — the language that is appropriate to the activity.

The teacher's task, then, is to design classroom activities that will, by their very nature, elicit the five language functions. For example, when we invite a small group to work on a mural to illustrate a social studies project, we will likely elicit language used to control and inform. To carry out the assignment, students will need to make statements such as, "Pass me the red crayon (controlling)," "We should put trees in the right-hand corner (controlling)," and "The covered wagons that crossed the prairies had smaller wheels (informing)." During the activity, students will, of course, use language for other purposes, but most of their talk will focus on controlling and informing. These are the functions that are appropriate to this activity.

When planning activities to elicit specific language functions, it's a good idea to keep in mind the underlying essence of the activity — the specific element at the core of the activity that can be generalized and applied to other similar activities. For example, when we suggest that members of a group make a mural, we are really asking them to work together to plan and create a tangible product. The same thing could be accomplished by inviting them to make a model, create an artifact, draw a picture, make a map and so on. As group members work on any of these assignments, they will use language to control and inform and, particularly in the planning stages, to forecast and reason.

An awareness of the underlying essence of various activities helps us create classroom situations designed to elicit language for various purposes.

Asserting and Maintaining Social Needs

One way of eliciting language for this function is to plan activities that require students to state their needs and negotiate with others.

We might, for example, suggest that students play games, such as checkers and chess, during their free time. Rather than providing a schedule for sharing the games, we can encourage interested students to work out a timetable of their own. To do so, they will need to state their needs, negotiate with others and establish how they are going to take turns. In the same way, students can be encouraged to develop their own schedule for using the classroom computers. Remember, the specifics of an activity are not the issue; it is the essence that is important.

Of course, we hope that students will meet their needs in positive rather than negative ways. However, should they be unable to do so, we can discuss acceptable behavior and how to negotiate politely as well as take turns. This provides us with an opportunity to model the positive aspects of this language function.

It is important to integrate these activities into the existing curriculum. For example, in science, partners might share a microscope to examine slides or a small group might share a magnet as members work together to discover the properties of magnets.

Controlling

If we wish to focus on language used to control, we may decide to provide partners or small groups with specific directions for creating something. While these directions may be written or oral, they can also be visual. Visual directions provide something students can see but don't necessarily involve words. For example, we may present students with a picture or model of something and ask them to replicate it. Oral directions are the least satisfactory because of their transitory nature. Students can refer back to written or visual directions.

Following directions, whether they are oral, written or visual, with a partner or small group requires students to focus on using language to control. For example, we might provide a model of a black cat at Halloween and invite students to make one just like it. The drawback is, of course, that this doesn't encourage creativity.

If we want students to create their own black cat, more planning will be involved and the language functions elicited will expand to include controlling, informing, forecasting and reasoning. When selecting activities and deciding on their structure, then, we need to balance a variety of considerations.

Informing

Language used to inform involves sharing information. When teachers use questions and dialogue to elicit this function, students will usually answer even when they realize that the teacher already knows the answer. They understand that the teacher is asking test or display questions and they perceive these as appropriate for teacher-to-child talk structures.

If a student asks test or display questions in a meeting with a small group of peers, however, other group members often perceive this behavior as inappropriate. In general, students don't ask each other display questions except when they are, for example, imitating the teacher or playing school. This means that, to elicit language used to inform during group activities, we must create situations in which questions are genuine and in which the speaker has a real need to share information with others.

In the primary grades, show-and-tell provides an excellent opportunity to do this. Because children often relate experiences that happened outside school, others in the class usually did not participate and this increases their interest. If children are encouraged to question the speaker afterwards, genuine questions are asked.

After reading a book, preferably one that is new to others in the class, older students can present a short book talk and field questions. Students can also share a piece of writing and answer questions about it.

Interviews designed to gather data for a unit of study are also excellent vehicles for eliciting language used to inform. Students can create questions and interview someone in the school or community, then report back to the class. Oral reports on topics others haven't studied are also useful.

Forecasting and Reasoning

To encourage students to use language to forecast and reason, activities must present a problem to be anticipated or solved or both. Science experiments are particularly good vehicles for eliciting this language function.

In addition to science experiments, problems that require students to list possible solutions, then narrow the list of possibilities also serve this purpose. For example, I might say to the class, "We need to give our parent volunteers a party at the end of the year. We'll need refreshments, decorations, and perhaps some entertainment. What should we do?" The students' suggestions would likely be listed during a brainstorming session. Then, as they begin to narrow down the alternatives, they will use language to forecast and reason.

Projecting

When students use language to project, they are injecting themselves into the experiences of others, whether these are people, animals or even inanimate objects.

An obvious activity for accomplishing this is role playing. Several children may get together to role play a scene from a novel, video, film or other material that has been presented to the class. For young children, a dress-up center can help elicit language for this function. When children put on costumes and pick up props, playing a role seems to occur naturally.

Assessing Use of Oral Language

Once we have planned and engaged students in activities, we will probably want to determine whether they are using the five language functions appropriately in a variety of situations. To do this accurately, we need to listen to students talk, decide what functions are being used, and relate the appropriateness of both the functions and the form in which they're expressed to the situation.

LISTEN TO STUDENTS TALK

Because it's easier to observe students when they are engaged in child-to-child or child-to-small group talk structures than during a teacher-led, whole-class discussions, it's a good idea to set the stage for this assessment by planning an activity for partners or small groups.

When planning activities for partners or small groups, we must consider the kind of language that is likely to be elicited in a given situation. For example, we would not listen to a student engaged in an activity designed to elicit language used to control and expect to hear language used to project. In this context, it would be incorrect to assume that the student is having problems using language for projecting. For this reason, we need to assess students in a variety of situations designed to elicit language used for a variety of functions.

While most activities will necessarily involve using language for asserting and maintaining social needs, controlling and informing, language used to forecast and reason as well as language used to project is more likely to be heard during activities designed specifically for these purposes.

Once the group activities are under way, the teacher can observe, making anecdotal notes about the language used and its appropriateness to the situation. It's best to concentrate on one group rather than to try to listen to the entire class during a single activity session.

ANALYZE FUNCTIONS

Before accurate anecdotal notes can be made, we need to get the hang of listening to students talk and deciding how they are using language. This requires practice.

While the following exercise is too time-consuming to be carried out regularly, it provides excellent practice in identifying the various language functions. Once you run through it two or three times, you'll develop the awareness necessary to make accurate observations about how individual students are using language.

The idea of this exercise is to separate language into manageable segments, then categorize them according to function. The easiest way to begin is to organize and record an activity involving no more than three students. Afterwards, prepare a written transcript of the tape or a segment of the tape. Because oral language is fleeting, it's helpful to be able to refer to the transcript.

Oral language is a continuous flow of thought translated into speech. To analyze how it is used, however, we must break it down into identifiable chunks. The transcript helps us do this.

An oral report, for example, is clearly too large a chunk. Over the course of presenting the report, students may use language for a variety of purposes. A single word, on the other hand, is clearly too small. The middle position, an utterance of an idea, is probably just right for our purposes. I call these utterances statements — short segments of talk that can be identified according to the following criteria:

- Clearly contain a thought or idea (e.g., "I'm going home now," "Do you have one?" and "Yes," and "No," in response to questions).
- Need not be grammatical in the formal sense (e.g., "Got it!" is as much a statement as "I have it!").
- Can be composed of a word, a series of words, or a complete sentence (e.g., "Run," when used as a command, "On the hook," in response to the question, "Where shall I put it?" and "I need $5.00," are all statements).
- Immediate repetition of a statement is not counted as two statements (e.g., "Lemme see, lemme see," is one statement).

The following transcript was prepared after recording a conversation between two kindergarten children as they worked in the cooking center to create a simple dish. A slash (/) designates statements:

Ann: Get the milk./

Carl: Where is it?/

Ann: On the table, on the table./

Carl: This is too lumpy./

Ann: (Critically) Well, if you would stir it harder and add more milk, it wouldn't be./ You're dumb./

Carl: I am not./

Before we proceed to categorize the statements identified in this conversation into the five language functions, we must deal with one more problem. Consider Ann's statement: "Well, if you would stir it harder and add more milk, it wouldn't be." Is she using language to assert and maintain social needs (criticizing) or to forecast and reason (cause and effect)? To answer, we must look beyond the actual words spoken and the context of two children preparing a dish at the cooking center. We must also consider tone of voice and facial features, body language and gestures. In addition, surrounding discourse may also provide clues to the speaker's purpose for using language.

After making this statement, Ann said, "You're dumb," and Carl responded, "I am not." Taking into account Ann's tone of voice and the surrounding dialogue, it seems fairly clear that her statement was used primarily to assert and maintain social needs, and perhaps secondarily to forecast and reason. In our categorization scheme, we'll concentrate on the primary function of the speaker's statements. Let's categorize the statements in the same transcript according to the function of the language used.

Ann: Get the milk./ (Controlling)

Carl: Where is it?/ (Informing)

Ann: On the table, on the table./ (Informing)

Carl: This is too lumpy./ (Informing)

Ann: (Critically) Well, if you would stir it harder and add more milk, it wouldn't be./ (Asserting and maintaining social needs) You're dumb./ (Asserting and maintaining social needs)

Carl: I am not./ (Asserting and maintaining social needs)

Once we feel confident about using this system of categories, we can observe three or four students a day and make anecdotal records about their use of language. These records won't provide an absolutely accurate count of the statements used for each language function, but this degree of precision is not needed in the classroom. They will give us a general notion, illustrated by examples of specific statements, of how students use language. Using a form similar to this may be helpful:

Student's Name _____

Date _____

Context (Description of Activity):

Other Students Engaging in the Activity:

Function Examples:

Function appropriate to the context? Yes _____ No _____

Form of function appropriate to the context? Yes _____ No _____

Recommendations for changes:

While the transcript of the conversation between the two children at the cooking center is too short to allow us to reach any definitive conclusions about their use of language, it will, nevertheless, help illustrate the need to analyze the appropriateness of function and form.

Because the two children are in a situation that calls for them to produce something, we can expect to hear language used to control and, perhaps, inform. We don't expect, however, to hear much language used to assert and maintain social needs or to project. If our observations of this and other similar situations reveal that a particular child spends a great deal of time criticizing others or justifying herself, we can conclude that language is not being used appropriately. We note this on the form and make recommendations for change. These may include assigning the child a different partner, speaking with her before the activity begins to make sure the directions are clear, or asking her to join two other children who will model appropriate language while the task is being carried out.

At the same time, even if the function is appropriate to the situation, the form in which the function is expressed may be inappropriate. For example, if I'm speaking to one of my children at home, it may be appropriate for me to say, "Please shut the door." If, on the other hand, I'm in a meeting with the president of the university, this form is likely inappropriate. I might say instead, "Do you mind if I shut the door?" "Could we shut the door?" or "I would prefer it if we shut the door." I may even say, "It's a bit cold in here."

In each case, I am using language to control, but the form is different. While criticizing and calling names may be normal for children in kindergarten, we want to help them move away from doing this. For example, it might have been more productive if Ann had said, "Maybe we could stir it harder and add more milk." Saying, "You're dumb," was entirely unnecessary. These are notes we can make when judging whether the form is appropriate. When considering recommendations for changes, we may wish to note that we will talk to the children about making remarks like this to others.

If students are observed two or three times during each reporting period, this information can help assess their use of language.

Responding to Children's Interests and the Curriculum

As previously mentioned, oral language activities should not be designed for the sole purpose of eliciting language for a particular function. Rather, they should complement and be integrated into the day-to-day life of the classroom. For example, choosing a kid of the week is routine in one classroom. Because this involves children in sharing experiences with others who weren't present at the time, it tends to elicit a great deal of language used to inform.

Every Friday, a draw is held to select the kid of the week. As names are drawn, they are eliminated from the pool so that every child has at least one turn. On Monday, the kid of the week brings to school six photographs of himself at various ages. These are mounted on a large piece of chart paper while he tells the class about each. Based on what the child says, appropriate captions are written under the pictures. The teacher records his name, address, and birthdate on the chart, along with his interests and hobbies.

The child then prepares a short oral autobiography and presents it to the class on Wednesday. In response, members of the class ask questions and are invited to draw a picture for or write a note to the kid of the week. These are placed on the chart. Before the kid of the week takes the chart home on Friday, his classmates give the teacher a list of things they like about him and these are included on the chart. This is a continuing activity, planned for a number of reasons — to promote self-esteem and develop friendships as well as to elicit informing language.

Activities can also arise directly from the curriculum. For example, as part of a study of ancient Greece, one grade seven class was working on the legend of the Minotaur. The teacher provided many resource materials, including several copies of the legend of the Minotaur and a picture of the palace at Knossos. A videotape describing the labyrinth was shown. After this information was presented, students were asked to choose a topic for a project. The topics included:

- With a partner, draw a labyrinth puzzle on chart paper with the Minotaur at its center (will elicit language used to control).
- Prepare an explanation for the class of the purpose of the labyrinth according to the legend (will elicit language used to inform).
- Tell the legend from the point of view of Theseus and then retell it from the point of view of King Minos (will elicit language used to project).

Whether these activities are part of the continuing classroom routine, such as kid of the week, or part of a unit of study, they respond to both students' interests and the curriculum. It is unnecessary to plan extra activities to elicit specific language functions; rather, it is a matter of considering the language functions and restructuring our current activities to include the ideas presented in this chapter.

By considering language functions when organizing classroom activities, we provide students with opportunities to use language for these functions and to hear it used in a variety of situations. We help children understand what language does, hear it in action, and see the results. We give form and substance to Michael Halliday's claim that children know what language is because they know what language does. We take one more step towards empowering children through language.

. . . .

LISTENING

Listening is, of course, integral to the talk structures and activities we've discussed so far. However, because listening is such an important topic — and one so often neglected — I've chosen to devote a separate chapter to it.

Because students spend so much of their school day listening to others and because the ability to listen well is an important asset for adults, listening may be the most important of the language arts. In 1928, Paul Rankin reported that adults spent 42.1 per cent of their time listening, 31.9 per cent speaking, 15 per cent reading and 11 per cent writing. Today, when reading printed material is losing ground to watching television, the percentage of time adults spend listening has probably climbed even higher. In 1950, Miriam Wilt found that elementary school students spent 60 per cent of the school day listening. This percentage has not changed appreciably since then. Listening is important, if for no other reason than that we spend so much time doing it.

Clearly, adequate listening skills are essential to learning content and functioning successfully in the classroom; indeed, listening is fundamental to all forms of communication. As students listen, they experience language, become acquainted with concepts and ideas, and develop vocabulary to use in speaking, reading and writing.

In *Listening: Its Impact at All Levels on Reading and Other Language Arts*, Sarah Lundsteen defines listening as the process by which spoken language is converted to meaning in the mind. And in *Listening Instruction*, Andrew Wolvin and Carolyn Coakley outlined the process like this:

Stimulus
→ Stimulus Is Received → Stimulus Is Attended to
→ Meaning Is Assigned → Meaning Is Remembered

For the listening process to swing into action, there must be a stimulus. We must be able to hear it, we must pay attention to it rather than blocking it while attending to other stimuli, we must be able to make sense of it, and we must remember the meaning we assigned to it.

In classrooms, we can ensure that this process operates smoothly by providing a variety of listening experiences, ensuring that students are able to hear, making the experiences interesting and stimulating for students, and, at the same time, equipping students with strategies for and providing practice in making meaning and remembering that meaning.

Listening has often been misunderstood and practiced ineffectively in schools because of a general belief that good listening habits come naturally to everybody whose hearing is adequate and a notion that listening can be taught outside the context of meaningful language. Meaningful language is language used for genuine communication within the context of actual classroom situations.

Listening is an active process of constructing meaning and, for this to happen, listeners need active mental involvement. While good instruction and lots of practice can help improve listening skills, this won't happen without meaningful talk in the classroom. Students listen more carefully if ideas are presented in interesting and relevant contexts and they have a real purpose for listening. Their interest and perception of a real purpose are stimulated best if listening is integrated into day-to-day classroom activities rather than presented in the form of isolated exercises.

If we find that students are not paying attention during a listening activity, one or more of the following factors may be operating:

— There is poor motivation to listen because the topic is not of interest and the student does not consider the information useful. This is more likely to happen when the listening experience is isolated rather than related to continuing classroom activities.
— The teacher talks too much and the students simply tune out.

- There are excessive distractions, such as too much noise or too many interruptions.
- The mental set for anticipating the speaker's message is missing. This is usually caused by a lack of previous knowledge about either the topic or the reason for listening. If we want students to listen for a particular reason, such as to list the causes of a particular event, we should tell them this before the listening experience takes place.

Students develop their listening skills through the give-and-take of discussions and by participating in a variety of activities. If we make an effort to establish a variety of talk structures — teacher-to-large or small group, child-to-adult, child-to child, child-to-small group and child-to-large group — they will have plenty of opportunities to practice both speaking and listening.

Finally, it's worth noting that students listen more carefully when they feel free to express ideas without fear of criticism or humiliation and when they have actively participated in formulating rules for listening experiences.

Teaching Listening

In *Thinking through the Language Arts*, Denise Nessel, Margaret Jones and Carol Dixon suggest three important elements of teaching listening to which I have added a fourth. These are:

- Providing a good role model.
- Establishing a conducive environment.
- Designing a program that includes many and varied listening experiences with different purposes and audiences.
- Providing direct instruction, when appropriate, within the context of genuine classroom activities.

PROVIDING A GOOD ROLE MODEL

We have already discussed how important it is for the teacher to listen attentively to students to help establish a healthy and productive psychological environment.

Another purpose for listening to students as they speak is to model good listening behavior. For example, when students present oral reports to the class, do we show that we are truly interested by listening carefully or do we take this opportunity to mark papers or engage in other activities? If appropriate, do we respond to the speaker with questions and comments that reflect our attention to what was said? As we join a small-group discussion, do we make eye contact with the speaker and truly listen to and value what is said? As we confer with individual students, do we give our undivided attention? In all these situations, we have an opportunity to model good listening behavior.

By establishing rules for listening activities and arranging the classroom to accommodate many and varied talk structures, we can provide an excellent environment for listening. The physical arrangement of the classroom and the necessity of establishing rules were discussed earlier. Nevertheless, it may be helpful to list rules specific to certain listening experiences. Here are two examples:

Child-to Large Group

Maintain eye contact with the speaker.
Do not speak unless recognized by speaker.
Raise hand and wait to be called on.
Do not engage in other activities, such as drawing, while someone is speaking.
If recognized by the speaker, ask questions or make comments relevant to what has been said.

Child-to-Small Group or Partner

Maintain eye contact with the speaker.
Wait your turn before speaking.
Be on topic or task.

In addition to establishing rules and organizing the physical environment, it's a good idea to check our own speaking behavior to make sure our speech is free of distractions that might cause listening problems. Unpleasant mannerisms, such as pacing or clearing the throat, and unfortunate habits, like speaking in a monotone, can distract and irritate listeners. Teaching is such a complex act that it's difficult to examine our own behavior while concentrating on the lesson, observing learners and enforcing rules. Videotaping ourselves or asking a fellow teacher to observe can often help us detect — and correct — flaws.

DESIGNING A PROGRAM

When designing a program, we must recognize the need to provide many and varied listening experiences with different purposes and audiences. These experiences will not be designed to teach and practice listening skills in isolation. Rather, they will integrate listening into day-to-day classroom activities. Listening occurs when students experience a piece of literature, learn about the world around them, follow directions to complete a project, and enjoy a piece of music.

The need to attend to the stimulus varies with the purpose for listening. Students may not need to attend as carefully when listening to music for enjoyment as when listening to a math word problem for the purpose of remembering critical facts.

To a great extent, the purpose for listening determines the listening strategies needed. Authorities such as Andrew Wolvin, Carolyn Coakley and Karin Porat list the following purposes for listening:

— Discriminative listening: Listening to distinguish sounds.
— Comprehensive listening: Listening to understand a message.
— Therapeutic listening: Listening to allow a speaker to talk through a problem.
— Critical listening: Listening to comprehend and evaluate a message.
— Appreciative listening: Listening for enjoyment.

In the classroom, comprehensive listening, critical listening and appreciative listening are probably used most frequently.

Of course, certain conditions are necessary if listening is to happen. The first is auditory acuity, or the physiological ability to hear. The second is auditory perception, or the ability to distinguish and remember sounds. Auditory perception tests evaluate one or more of the following crucial factors: the ability to distinguish one sound from another; the blending of sounds; and the ability to remember sounds and repeat them in sequence.

If we, as classroom teachers, suspect that a student has a problem with auditory acuity or perception, it is our responsibility to refer the child to the school nurse or the district's speech and hearing therapist for testing. In *Listening: Its Impact at All Levels on Reading and Other Language Arts*, Sarah Lundsteen pinpoints signs for teachers to watch for:

— Frequent requests for repetition during oral exercises.
— Rubbing of ears.
— Poor pronunciation.
— Daydreaming or lack of attention during oral activities.

Discriminative listening is certainly important, but students with normal auditory acuity and perception usually don't need extensive practice in this type of listening. Therapeutic listening is also important, but is normally not as necessary in school settings as in other situations. In classrooms, it is more often needed by the teacher rather than the students. For these reasons, I will concentrate on comprehensive listening, critical listening and appreciative listening.

Comprehensive Listening

It's important to expose students to listening in a variety of audience settings. This can be accomplished by organizing a variety of talk structures in the classroom. For example, when students listen to different partners or different members of a small group, or to the teacher or another student making an oral presentation to the class, the nature of their participation in an audience changes. The following activities provide further opportunities to vary the audience setting:

— Invite guest speakers to the classroom.
— Show films or TV programs.
— Use field trips to attend lectures, plays or oral presentations.
— Engage the class in cross-age tutoring or a buddy system where, for example, a grade six student is paired with a grade two student for 30 minutes a week to read and talk about books.

- Invite students to interview, either in person or over the telephone, members of the community in conjunction with a school project.

Directed listening-thinking activities, or DLTAs, described by Russell Stauffer, are excellent vehicles for encouraging comprehensive and critical thinking. They are similar to directed reading-thinking activities, except that the focus is exclusively on oral language. DLTAs foster creative and logical thinking and provide practice in listening carefully for information and details. In *Language Arts: Learning Processes and Teaching Practices*, Charles Temple and Jean Gillett, set out the steps of a DLTA:

- Select an interesting story with an obvious plot structure and appealing illustrations. Fairy tales and folk tales are often useful because they have clear-cut elements of conflict or attempts to achieve a goal as well as a clear resolution.
- Show the listeners the cover of the book and talk about the title. Ask them to predict what the story might be about.
- Plan to stop reading two to four times during the story, preferably before an important event occurs or important information is revealed. Don't stop too many times as frequent stops can fragment the story, causing listeners to lose interest.
- At each stopping point, ask a student to summarize what has happened so far. If the story is long or complicated, one student may start this summary, a second may pick up where the first left off, and so on. Afterwards, invite predictions about what will happen next and why.
- Accept all predictions without making judgments. The point is to develop logical alternatives rather than to be right. Use terms such as "likely" or "unlikely" rather than "right" and "wrong."
- When confirming predictions, focus on the idea rather than the person who volunteered the idea.
- Keep discussions short and to the point. Get back to the story before students' interest wanes.
- You may wish to plan a response afterwards. For example, small or large groups might discuss the predic-

tions. Could they have worked out? Why? This activity asks students to draw upon personal experience and listen carefully for details.

A word of caution! While research indicates that comprehension is enhanced if listeners are invited to respond both during and after listening experiences, we need to remember that many stories are meant simply to be read and enjoyed. If you read to students every day, you may wish to do a DLTA only once or twice a week. Or, you may wish to make the DLTA a separate experience from the literature you read aloud daily. A DLTA is a valuable experience, but children shouldn't feel as if they must always respond to things that are read aloud. Let's try to avoid the I-don't-want-to-read-a-book-if-I-have-to-write-a-book-report syndrome.

The inquest technique, set out by Mary Shoop in an article in *The Reading Teacher*, also fosters comprehensive and critical listening. This technique asks students to respond during and after listening experiences.

— Choose a story to read aloud. This activity works best if the characters are well-developed and the story builds to a strong climax.
— As students listen, they are to choose one character and think of questions to ask him or her.
— Stop at a critical point and ask students to write down their questions.
— Divide the class into small groups whose members all chose the same character and invite them to role play a news conference. Three or four students can be news reporters while one student plays the character. The reporters ask questions and the character answers based on information from the story to that point.
— Read to another critical point, stop and repeat the procedure. Within the small group, students change roles.
— Finish the story and repeat the process.
— Afterwards, the interviews can be evaluated. Students can brainstorm to come up with other questions they might have asked. They can also evaluate whether the character's answers were based on information in the story and, if not, decide what the character might have said.

If we believe that the meaning of a particular passage or poem is not found exclusively in the text but rather depends on a complex interaction between the reader and the text, it becomes important for us to encourage students to respond personally to literature.

After a listening experience, students can respond in writing or orally, in either small groups or a large group. To facilitate their responses, we can ask open-ended questions such as, "What did you like?" "What did you dislike?" "What do you wonder about?" Questions like these encourage students to articulate their personal feelings about a passage rather than requiring them to come up with a list of facts or information.

They may also respond by selecting and drawing a scene, character, or event that held particular significance for them, making up questions — real questions that they genuinely wonder about — that they would like to ask a character, or comparing a character with one in a different story. Most language arts teaching guides suggest a variety of activities designed to encourage students to respond to a piece of literature.

When the school bus is late or we're waiting for an assembly to begin, it's handy to have a supply of language games to fill in the time — and promote listening comprehension. I particularly like mental math and Queen Anne because they involve creativity and the answers are different every time they're played.

To play mental math, the teacher lists orally a series of numbers and operations and asks students to supply the answer. The difficulty can vary with the age group. For example, we might say, "What's 3 times 4, divided by 6, times 10, minus 5." Students must work out the answer — 15. To do so, they must listen carefully, because missing an element makes it impossible to arrive at an answer. In a large group, it's sometimes helpful if everyone responds individually in writing before one student is called on to supply the answer.

Queen Anne begins with a story. We might say, "Queen Anne is coming to our city and, to prepare for her visit, we must discover what she likes. Listen and see if you can figure it out. Queen Anne likes jelly but not jam. Queen Anne likes green but not blue. Queen Anne likes skiing but not skating. Queen Anne likes running but not walking."

During this particular session, Queen Anne likes only things that have a double letter — jelly, green, skiing, etc. Once a student figures this out, she supplies her own example for the teacher to confirm. This avoids giving away the answer and keeps others interested in figuring it out. For example, if the student said, "Queen Anne likes sheets but not bedspreads," the teacher would say, "Yes, that's right." On the other hand, if the student said, "Queen Anne likes paper but not pencils," the teacher would say, "No, I don't think so," and provide another example.

The game continues until several students have solved the problem. The teacher then calls on one of them to reveal what causes Queen Anne to like something.

The next time the game is played, the criterion for winning Queen Anne's approval changes. For example, Queen Anne might like butterflies but not bees, gumdrops but not licorice, and so on. This time, the criterion is compound words.

This game has endless possibilities and can be matched to the age level of the children. Like mental math, Queen Anne encourages students to listen carefully for details.

Critical Listening

Critical listening involves evaluating and interpreting something that was heard. To encourage critical listening, teachers might ask questions like, "Should the character behave that way?" "Is that realistic?" or "Would I have written it that way if I were the author?" To evaluate a piece of literature critically, listeners must understand and be involved with it, both intellectually and emotionally.

Inviting students to respond to literature is an excellent way to stimulate critical listening. After a reading, we can model making statements such as "I don't like what that character did because it didn't seem to fit with his earlier behavior. What do you think?" or "I think it's all right to lie in certain circumstances if I know the lie will save somebody pain or embarrassment, but what do you think?"

Encouraging students to evaluate things they hear takes modeling, opportunity and practice, but it produces true involvement with literature. To help formulate questions and comments that encourage critical listening, it may be helpful to review a taxonomy of questions such as Bloom's, which was set out in the chapter titled Talk Structures. A word of caution, however. When referring to a taxonomy, guard against composing questions that reflect the taxonomy, but ignore the literature. Remember, we are attempting to develop students' interest in literature. Over the course of the school year, we will probably read a variety of literature. Some of the works will lend themselves to this kind of evaluation more readily than others. Remember to provide students with plenty of opportunities to listen for enjoyment as well.

When students listen to materials designed to impart information, it's necessary to distinguish between fact and opinion. I remember that my own children, at the ages of 13 and 14, believed that things were true simply because they heard them on television. This is a common misconception, even among students beyond elementary school. If we expose students to information that contains both facts and opinion, we can help them establish criteria for distinguishing between the two.

By the same token, it's also necessary for students to realize that facts can be slanted to suit an author's purpose and point of view. For example, is it likely that an article on gun control written by a member of the National Rifle Association will present the facts in an unbiased way? Newspapers are effective resources for developing students' awareness of bias. Several different articles and letters to the editor on the same topic can be collected and examined. Students can then discuss why they contain the information they do. Developing these skills is an important part of learning to listen or read critically.

When we engage in appreciative listening, we are listening for enjoyment. It's worth noting that it's often difficult to draw firm boundaries between comprehensive listening, critical listening and appreciative listening. We are unlikely to enjoy something if we don't understand it and, in most instances, the more we enjoy something, the more we're motivated to understand and evaluate it. For example, when attending a play, we may listen for entertainment, but we also listen for information because a certain amount of information is necessary for us to be entertained. At the age of 11, I saw a Shakespearean play that I didn't enjoy at all because I couldn't understand it. Listening to music may be an exception to this, because it is certainly possible to enjoy it while knowing little about it.

In the classroom, the distinction between appreciative listening and other kinds of listening lies not so much in the listening experience itself, but in what we expect students to do during and after the experience. If we ask them to listen strictly for enjoyment, we are unlikely to demand a response unless they wish to make one. Do we ever read aloud a good book, close the cover and let students savor it silently, or do we always expect students to discuss it, write a different ending, or role play one of the characters? If we wish to encourage them to listen for enjoyment, we must sometimes close the cover and allow them to savor!

Instructional Strategies

We've looked at various purposes for listening as well as specific activities that provide students with opportunities for practice. In *Language Arts Content and Teaching Strategies*, Kenneth Hoskisson and Gail Tompkins list several strategies that can enhance students' ability to listen. These strategies can be applied in a wide range of situations.

CREATING IMAGES

If a speaker's message contains many visual images, details, or descriptive words, it's often helpful for listeners to create an image or picture in their mind. We can help students develop this ability by stopping part way through a film, story or poem and asking them to create a mental picture based on what they heard. It helps to model this by sharing our own mental image and asking various students to do the same.

WEBBING

If information is clustered, this often provides a useful framework for improving listening comprehension. Constructing a web that indicates relationships is a good way to cluster information because it's easier to understand and remember ideas that are related rather than presented as a series of unrelated facts. After a listening experience, we can work with students to construct a web on the chalkboard. While making the web, try asking why each idea is placed in a particular spot.

Here's an example of a web developed to help students remember information about pigeons:

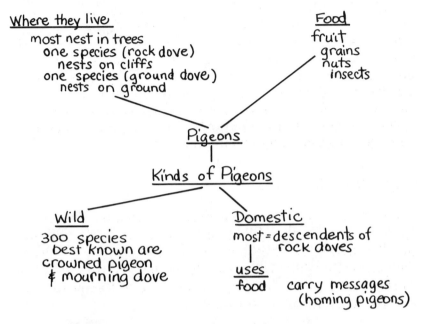

ASKING QUESTIONS

It's helpful if listeners ask two kinds of questions during listening experiences: those directed to the speaker to help clarify a message and those directed to oneself to monitor whether the material is making sense.

To encourage students to ask the first kind of question, we can stop during listening experiences and ask them if they have questions for the speaker. This works particularly well during films or taped presentations because these can be started and stopped at will. To model the process, we can share our own questions.

Questions designed to monitor our own understanding can be handled the same way. At appropriate points during a film, for example, we can stop and say things like, "What questions are you asking yourself at this point? Here is what I'm asking myself."

Speakers usually structure their messages in four predictable patterns: description-enumeration, sequence, comparison-contrast and cause-effect. These patterns can be pointed out to students in the hope that, with practice, they will recognize them as they listen. This often makes it easier for them to organize and remember ideas.

A speaker who chooses to use the description-enumeration pattern usually recites a series of facts about a topic, all of which are equally important. Here's an example:

"Haida Indians once occupied the Queen Charlotte Islands of British Columbia and part of Prince of Wales Island in Alaska. They lived by fishing, hunting and collecting wild plants. Haida communities included highly organized clans, social classes, secret societies, and hereditary nobility. The upper classes possessed much wealth in the form of slaves and fishing grounds. The Haida excelled in various crafts common to the Pacific Northwest, including canoe- and house-building as well as wood-carving."

Speakers may also choose to present a series of events in sequence. This may include specific dates, as in the following example, or simply relate one event after another.

"Canada's first school was probably opened in Quebec in 1620. That year, Madame Samuel de Champlain, the wife of the famous explorer, began teaching French and the Roman Catholic religion to a group of natives. The Jesuit College of Quebec, for French and native boys, was founded in 1635. The Ursuline Convent school for girls was established in Quebec in 1639. English language schools were set up in various parts of Canada in the mid-1700s."

Speakers who use the comparison-contrast pattern compare an idea or event with another. Here's an example:

"There are six main breeds of beef cattle in North America. Of these, Charolais and Santa Gertrudis are probably the most popular. Charolais were originally bred in France, while Santa Gertrudis originated in the United States. The former are distinctively white in color, while the latter are reddish brown. Another distinguishing feature is size, as Charolais are normally larger than Santa Gertrudis."

Finally, speakers may use the cause-effect pattern, illustrated by the following example:

"Anthrax is a serious disease that attacks cattle, especially dairy cattle. Anthrax is caused by a germ that is usually picked up from the soil. This germ enters the animal's body through the mouth. Anthrax causes a high fever and often stops the flow of milk. It is extremely dangerous to cattle and is often fatal."

Teachers can help students recognize these patterns by:

— Initiating: Explain the patterns and the kinds of activities for which each is effective. Introduce one pattern at a time.
— Structuring: Choose and explain a topic using a particular pattern. As part of the process, create appropriate graphic organizers — webs, semantic maps, Venn diagrams, charts, etc. — on the chalkboard. Remember to discuss one pattern completely before introducing a second. It may be necessary to repeat the process several times before students understand. Here's a chart that might be used when explaining the comparison-contrast pattern:

Charolais	Santa Gertrudis
Originated in France	Originated in U.S.
Color — white	Color — reddish brown
Larger in size	Smaller in size

— Conceptualizing: After explaining the various patterns one at a time and illustrating them with graphic organizers, suggest a number of topics and invite students to create their own example of a pattern, including a graphic organizer, and explain it to a partner.
— Generalizing: After all the patterns have been demonstrated and constructed by the students, read aloud a passage and ask students to determine the pattern and construct a graphic organizer.

While the suggested examples may certainly be used to demonstrate a pattern, we should try to use information that students actually need in a learning situation. Students should not be asked to carry out isolated listening activities for the sole purpose of practicing listening skills. Rather, listening should be presented as a genuine strategy for learning needed information.

A Word about Assessment

Listening is assessed most effectively within the context of meaningful classroom experiences. The teacher's observations during learning situations are probably the most effective means of assessing listening ability. The following is an example of a combined rating scale and anecdotal record form that can be used to assess listening. Feel free to revise the checklist by adding other listening skills and strategies that are pertinent to your classroom.

Listening Checklist

Student's Name _____

Rating

5=Always 4=Usually 3=Sometimes 2=Rarely 1=Never

Characteristic	Date/Comment	Date/Comment
Pays attention to oral presentations		
Enjoys listening to stories and poems		
Listens without interruption		
Follows oral directions		
Responds appropriately to various listening experiences		

"DOING" ORAL LANGUAGE

IN THE CLASSROOM

As I've already stressed, oral language skills are learned best when they are integrated into regular classroom activities rather than presented in isolation. Using oral language — both speaking and listening — provides children with a valuable tool both for learning in all subject areas and for dealing with the daily chores and activities that are part of classroom life.

When thinking about broadening students' exposure to oral language, teachers must take into account two considerations that lie at the core of teaching and learning in every classroom. The first is content — the subject matter we plan to teach — and the second is the overall method of classroom organization — how we structure learning situations throughout the school day.

The content we plan to teach is determined by a number of factors, including the needs, interests and abilities of the students in our classrooms, curriculum guidelines, and the availability of resource materials.

When we integrate oral language into our classrooms, it is unlikely to change the content we teach. It will, however, change the way this content is presented. For example, problem-solving in mathematics may now be done with partners rather than individually or students may work in small groups on a science experiment rather than watching the teacher demonstrate, then reading about it in a text. Students will have more freedom to interact orally with one another during what were previously quiet work periods. Because we recognize the value of peer teaching and interaction, we will loan some of our control to the students. Learning will become a social event rather than an individual activity. As these patterns shift, oral language will be emphasized in whatever content is appropriate to individual classrooms.

Classroom organization, the second pertinent consideration, remains up to individual teachers. Oral language can be integrated smoothly and effectively using any one of the three organizational patterns prevalent today: arranging content according to time blocks; incorporating content from various subject areas into themes; or building content-related experiences into learning stations or centers. These organizational methods are not mutually exclusive. Indeed, we may use more than one over the course of the school year and we may even use a combination of two or even three at any one time.

The key to encouraging oral language in the classroom is to introduce a variety of talk structures that correlate both to content and classroom organization. What follows is a guide to integrating oral language when using any one of the three methods of classroom organization. First is a typical day divided into time blocks, then a theme scheduled to last a week, and, finally, a series of learning centers designed to present content and elicit productive oral language. As you read, notice the talk structures that have been established. You can use these suggestions as a guide when planning talk structures to meet the needs of students in your own classroom.

Time Blocks

Grade 5

9:00-9:15 — Roll Call, Announcements and News

As students enter the classroom, they turn over an attendance card in a pocket chart. A student monitors this procedure and fills out an attendance report for the office. Class members are expected to go to their seats quietly and read or complete unfinished work until this process is over. After attendance has been taken, the "teacher of the day" makes announcements and students discuss new developments in the news story they are following. If anyone has brought in pictures or news articles, these are added to bulletin board designated for the news.

9:15-10:00 — Reading

On this particular day, a readers' workshop is planned. For the first 10 minutes, the teacher presents a mini-lesson to the whole class on a particular reading strategy, such as using context clues. She uses an overhead transparency to demonstrate, then questions the students. For the next five minutes, the teacher checks the status of the class. This technique, described by Nancie Atwell in *In the Middle: Reading, Writing and Learning with Adolescents*, involves a kind of roll call where students, in turn, tell the teacher what book they're reading, the page number they've reached, and discuss problems they may have encountered.

For the next 25 minutes, students silently read books they've chosen themselves from the class or school library. The teacher circulates, conferring with individual students and making notes on the status-of-the-class record sheet or other record form. The teacher discusses books with students, saying things like, "What part did you like best? Tell me a bit about that part," or "What do you think is about to happen? Why?" The teacher may ask students to be prepared to read a short passage aloud.

During the last five minutes of the period, two or three students present book talks to the whole class. This gives students an opportunity to share and celebrate good books, while encouraging others to read the book at a later date.

During this time on other days, the teacher may organize small-group discussions for students who have read similar kinds of books, such as animal stories, or different titles by the same author. These discussions can be held during the 25-minute silent reading time and need not involve all students. For example, two groups of five might discuss books while the rest of the class reads silently. The physical environment of the classroom has been considered, and there are areas for small groups to meet without disrupting others.

At various times during the school year, the teacher invites several students to read the same book at the same time. She provides five or six copies of three or four titles and, after reviewing each briefly, asks students to choose one. When several students read the same book, many small-group discussions and activities can be planned. The students keep response journals in preparation for these discussions. Occasionally, the teacher may ask students to discuss books from the point of view of one of the characters. This activity will elicit language used to project.

10:00-10:45 — Writing

This period is designated as a writers' workshop, another concept discussed by Nancie Atwell in *In the Middle: Reading, Writing and Learning with Adolescents*. For the first 10 minutes, the teacher presents a mini-lesson with demonstrations and questions. Afterwards, the status of the class is quickly checked, this time with respect to students' writing. As students' name are called, the teacher jots down the title of the piece they're working on and notes whether they're on a first draft, revision, second draft, and so on.

For the next 20 minutes, students write at their desks, confer informally with partners, or work at the typewriter or computer to publish a piece. The teacher circulates and provides individual help during writing conferences. During this time, students are free to discuss a piece of writing with a peer, ask a peer to listen to a portion of the writing, or seek advice. There are places in the classroom where students may go to work undisturbed.

For the last five minutes every day, one or two students share their writing with the whole class. While the teacher may ask students to share, whether they do so remains up to them. Often, students will themselves request an opportunity to share something with the class. After a piece of writing is shared, the author usually responds to questions from other class members.

10:45-10:55 — Recess

10:55-11:45 — Mathematics

Students work individually from a text and other prepared materials. During this work period, they are allowed to interact with other students and ask others for help if the teacher is not available. For the first five minutes, the teacher may use the chalkboard to present a concept, then respond to questions.

As the students work on their assignments, the teacher calls together *ad hoc* groups. Members of *ad hoc* groups get together for a short time, usually for no longer than a week, because of a common need or interest. For example, if eight students in the classroom needed help with dividing fractions, the teacher might call together an *ad hoc* group and provide instruction.

During the last 10 minutes of the work period, students check their answers with each other and jointly work out discrepancies.

11:45-12:00 — Clean-Up and Fine Arts Appreciation

The teacher may read aloud poetry, present prints by famous artists, or talk about well-known composers and play examples of their work. Sometimes, students present short oral biographies of famous writers, artists or composers. The class may study one particular poet, artist or composer for a period of days or weeks.

12:00-12:45 — Lunch

12:45-1:00 — Teacher reads aloud

1:00-2:00 — Physical Education, Music or Art (depending on the day of the week)

2:00-2:15 — Recess

2:15-2:50 — Social Studies

The class has been divided into small groups to study West Coast native peoples. Each group chooses one aspect of the culture, such as myths and legends or modes of transportation, and presents both a written report and an oral demonstration. Members of each group choose a topic, draw up preliminary plans and discuss these with the teacher, then decide how each member will contribute to the group effort.

During this period, students often work individually on their personal portion of the group project. The groups meet two to three times a week to check on the progress of individual members. Each group is responsible for teaching its topic to other members of the class and fielding questions asked during the oral presentation. Each group develops expertise on one particular topic and becomes a resource for the rest of the class. Portions of these oral presentations may include dramatizations or other forms of artistic work. Students know they will be assessed over the range of topics that have been presented.

2:50-3:20 — Science (three days a week) or Computer Instruction (two days)

Students work in small groups on particular topics within a unit to demonstrate what they know to others who have chosen a different topic.

3:20-3:30 — Clean-Up, Language Games, Announcements, Dismissal

In analyzing this day, note the variety of talk structures included in the activities. Students had many opportunities to talk to the teacher, work formally and informally with a partner and in small groups, and to talk in front of the whole group.

As the teacher planned these activities, she considered the functions of language. For example, as students reviewed books or presented reports, they used a great deal of language to inform. As they worked together in small groups to plan presentations, they used language to control and assert and maintain social needs. As they performed science experiments and attempted to figure out the best way of presenting a demonstration, they used language to forecast and reason. And, as they discussed books from the point of view of others and presented dramatizations as part of their social studies projects, they used language to project.

Themes

Grade One: Theme — Farm Animals

Instead of dividing the day into time blocks, reading, writing, oral language, science, social studies, art and music are integrated into various activities revolving around a farm animals theme.

Children enter the classroom eager to share the books they took home to share with their families the previous evening. While the teacher chats with individuals about these books, other children are encouraged to read quietly or work on their writing folders.

After the teacher has called the roll, he summons the class to the carpeted area. He has copied Meguido Zola's story, "I Bought Me a Cat," onto a chart and plans to use it as the basis for a shared reading experience. The story is about farm animals, including a pig, goose, horse and cow. The teacher introduces the story by saying, "We've read about a number of farm animals over the past few days. Let's see how many we can name." The children brainstorm to come up with a list that the teacher records on the chalkboard. He then says, "Which of these animals do you think will be in this story? Let's pick five."

After the children do so, the teacher reads the story aloud. He then reads it again, this time pointing to the words on the chart as he reads. Together, he and the children check the predictions to see if the five animals the children suggested are actually included in the story. As each animal is confirmed, a child comes up to the chart and points to the word in the story while the teacher places a checkmark beside the animal's name on the list.

In this story, each new animal is introduced with the line, "I bought me a..., my...pleased me." After the story has been read several times, the teacher presents a mini-lesson on the sounds produced by the letters "ea." Another mini-lesson on using a capital letter to begin a sentence and a period to end it is also presented. During each lesson, the teacher refers to the text of the story on the chart.

These mini-lessons are short and without any direct follow-up, as the teacher knows that some children are ready for these ideas while others are not. For those who are not, the lessons will be presented again throughout the school year.

After the shared reading experience and the mini-lessons, the children return to their desks to write and illustrate a short story about their favorite farm animal. This is a suggestion, not an assignment. The children know they can choose to write on any topic they wish. They are encouraged to consult with peers during writing time, and one group of three decides to work together on a long story about a magic rabbit. During this time, the teacher circulates, conferring with the children and providing individual help. As the children finish their writing, they choose books — fiction and non-fiction — from the classroom library or off a special table set up to display books about farm animals.

When the children return to the carpeted area for another whole-group session, three of them take turns reading their own stories aloud to the group and responding to questions.

The teacher often uses the content of the children's stories to develop mini-lessons on concepts and vocabulary. After the third child reads her writing and responds to questions, the teacher uncovers a secret message that had been hidden on the chalkboard. It reads as follows:

_ P_g i_ th_ t__ch__'s f_v_r___ f__ a__m_l. W__t i_ y___?
D_ y__ l____ c_w_ or d_ y__ l__ h____?

The children choose a partner and work together for a few minutes to figure out the message. Then the teacher works with the whole class to fill in the blanks. This is instructional time and the teacher draws attention to things such as the sounds of letters, punctuation and context clues. The message is translated quickly by the students:

A pig is the teacher's favorite farm animal. What is yours?
Do you like cows or do you like horses?

The teacher calls attention to the sound made by "ea" in "teacher," referring back to the story to find the "ea" in "pleased."

After deciphering the secret message, the children enjoy music and movement to the song, "The Farmer in the Dell." They then return to their desks to read a book of their choice, either silently or with a buddy. Copies of "I Bought Me a Cat" are available for those who choose to read it again and the story is also on tape at the listening post for those who would like to hear it again while they follow along in the book. For the next 10 or 15 minutes, the teacher confers with individual children, asking them about their book and requesting that they read part of it aloud.

After the conferences, a small *ad hoc* group is called to the carpeted area to review the story, "I Bought Me a Cat." This time, the teacher uses two pocket charts. For one, he has prepared sentence strips that read, "I bought me a cat," "I bought me a pig," "I bought me a horse," and so on. The other contains strips that read, "My pig said, 'Oink, oink,'" "My horse said, 'Neigh, neigh,'" and so on. The teacher invites the children to match the sentences contained in the two charts. This is done first as a shared reading experience, then individually.

After the sentences have been read several times, the teacher plays a simple tune on the piano and the children match the sentences in the pocket charts in the form of a song. As they sing, one child points to the words. This activity continues as a simple movement game in which the teacher, for example, holds up a card on which the word "cat" is printed. He chooses a child, who says, "Meow, meow," and mimes the actions of a cat.

When this activity is finished, the class is called to the carpeted area and three or four children are invited to tell about the books they are reading. Sometimes they read part of the book aloud to the group or share a choral reading.

Later, the children interview each other about their favorite farm animal, count the responses and then chart these on a simple bar graph. In the process, interview skills are discussed and graphing techniques are taught. The graph reveals that horses are the overwhelming favorite.

After lunch, the teacher reads aloud a story. Then the children move into their study groups. With the help of the school librarian, the teacher has filled the classroom with pictures, charts and books about farm animals. Many of the books are non-fiction and arranged in a special area. Each group chooses one farm animal. Using the resources and with the help of the teacher, the children find out as much as possible about the animal they chose and record this in their journals along with simple illustrations.

At the end of the day, each group reports one or two things they discovered to the class and the teacher records these findings on large charts at the front of the room. There is a chart for each animal and these are reviewed frequently to stress what the children already know and what still needs to be discovered. When the theme ends, the children can review everything they know about horses, cows, pigs and so on.

This thematic organization provides many opportunities for children to talk to the teacher, work formally and informally with partners, work in small groups and speak in front of the large group. The children use language for a variety of functions as they work with one another in a variety of settings.

Grade 7: Social Studies Centers on Ancient Greece

This particular class is organized into centers only for social studies. The teacher introduces the unit by screening a film on life in ancient Greece. This not only provides background information but can also be used to review listening strategies. After the film, the description-enumeration pattern for organizing information is discussed and a web is created on the chalkboard.

When using centers as an organizational structure, it is particularly important to choose activities carefully. Their success often depends heavily on the availability of resources.

When the unit began, students were assigned to a small group of five or six and will remain with this group for the duration of the unit. There are five centers set up on tables around the periphery of the classroom and the groups spend a week at each before rotating to the next. Materials and instructions for their use are included at each center, but students can use the materials anywhere in the classroom. At the end of the social studies period, all materials must be returned to the centers. Every Friday, the students complete group and individual evaluations.

CENTER ONE: Ancient Crete — Legend of the Minotaur

Materials: A videotape describing the labyrinth, pictures and charts, including a reproduction of the palace at Knossos, various books and materials about ancient Crete and the legend of the Minotaur.

Activities:

- View the videotape. Afterwards, appoint a secretary to take notes and a chairperson to lead the discussion. In your discussion, summarize the important points from the tape and record your impressions of life in ancient Crete. The secretary should turn in the notes on the discussion to the teacher.
- Study pictures and the reproduction of the palace at Knossos to find physical evidence of a labyrinth. Read the legend of the Minotaur in one of the books provided and choose one of the following activities:

a) With a partner, draw a labyrinth puzzle on chart paper with the Minotaur at the center. Invite another group member to solve the puzzle.

b) Prepare an oral explanation for the group on the purpose of the labyrinth according to the legend.

c) Rewrite the legend from the point of view of Theseus and then retell it orally from the point of view of King Minos. Practice your oral presentation with a partner, then tape it.

CENTER TWO: Sparta and Athens

Materials: Books and filmstrips on Sparta and Athens.

Activities:

— Divide up the research materials and prepare a written report comparing ancient Sparta and Athens. Each person in the group should pick one topic, such as government, education, military service, home life or contributions to the arts. On Friday, be prepared to meet with your group to share orally the information you've discovered. Do not read aloud your written report. Instead, find an interesting way to share the information with the others. You may wish to practice this with a partner in the same or a different group before making your presentation.

CENTER THREE: Greek Architecture

Materials: Pictures of Greek temples and buildings as they appeared in ancient times and pictures of the existing ruins, books and materials on the architecture of ancient Greece, as well as cardboard tubes, cardboard, styrofoam, paper and paints.

Activities:

— With a partner, make a model of the Parthenon from the materials available at the station. Upon completion, be prepared to present this model to your group and explain how it was made.

CENTER FOUR: The Olympic Games

Materials: Filmstrips and books on the ancient Olympics as well as material on the modern Olympics.

Activities:

Complete two of the following:

- Prepare a program for the ancient Olympic games. Include all the events and when they are to take place. Choose one of the events and be prepared to demonstrate it for your group.
- Compare either the modern discus or javelin throw with the ancient event. State the differences. Which event, ancient or modern, do you think requires greater skill? Explain your answer in writing and be prepared to demonstrate to your group.
- Find out how the Olympic torch was lit in ancient times and explain how this differs from modern times.
- Find out what sports were included in the ancient decathlon and explain how this differs from the modern event.

CENTER FIVE: Religion — Mythology

Materials: Pictures, books and filmstrips on Greek gods, goddesses and mythology.

Activities:

Choose one of the following. Be prepared to share your project orally with your group on Friday.

- With a partner, prepare a "family tree" showing the relationships of the gods and goddesses.
- Choose the god or goddess you found most interesting. Prepare a brief talk explaining what impressed you about this god or goddess.
- Choose your favorite Greek myth and retell it from the point of view of the god or goddess who is the main character.

These centers were organized to involve students actively in learning content and to stimulate the use of oral language in a variety of talk structures. As students worked at the centers, the teacher functioned as a facilitator, making suggestions, obtaining additional resources, providing information, and conferring with students about specific projects. During this time, the teacher also observed students and made anecdotal notes about how the work was progressing. All written products were to be turned in to the teacher to be checked and evaluated. If further, more formal assessment is needed or desired, students can be tested on all the material at the centers at the end of five weeks. This testing would be individual although they worked collaboratively to learn the material.

The activities suggested here are intended as examples only. If we are to integrate oral language successfully into our own classrooms programs, we must work with content that is unique to the needs of the students in our classes and with organizational patterns that allow us to feel comfortable. We must also be committed to the idea that oral language is a valuable learning tool.

I end this book as I began, with a story that is, in a very real sense, a sequel. My daughter, who is now in her early 20s, is a member of the strata council, or governing body, of her apartment building. One of the residents is suing the council to recover costs associated with repairing damage to his car that occurred as a result of an accident in the building's underground parking garage. Although my daughter is by far the youngest member of the council, she has volunteered to file the necessary documents and represent the group in small claims court. As she chatted with me about this project, I thought back to the many hours she had spent listening to my telephone conversations and accompanying me to court when I had my own brush with the law many years ago.

Perhaps I shouldn't be, but somehow I am amazed at her willingness and ability to take on this task. In light of her experience, I recognize anew that the desire to tap into the power of language is contagious. As we model this power for students and our own children and provide them with time and opportunities to use language, we show them, little by little, how to make it their own.

I challenge you to become committed to fostering the use of oral language in your classroom and to search for ways to make oral language an integral part of your school day. You *can* help students discover the power of language and make it their own. I want it for them — and I hope you do too!

. . . .

BIBLIOGRAPHY

Creating an Environment for Oral Language

Atwell, N. *In the Middle: Writing, Reading and Learning with Adolescents.* Portsmouth, New Hampshire: Boynton/Cook, 1987.

Blumenfeld, P. & J. Meece. "Life in Classrooms Revisited. In *Theory into Practice.* Vol. 24, No. 1 (1985).

Brophy, J. & T. Good. "Teacher Behavior and Student Achievement." In *Handbook of Research on Teaching,* 3rd Ed. (M. Whittrock, Ed.). New York: Macmillan, 1986.

Brophy, J. & C. Evertson. *Learning from Teaching; A Developmental Perspective.* Boston, Massachusetts: Allyn & Bacon, 1976.

Doyle, W. "Classroom Organization and Management." In *Handbook of Research on Teaching,* 3rd Ed. (M. Whittrock, Ed.). New York: Macmillan, 1986.

Eeds, M. & D. Wells. "Grand Conversations: An Exploration of Meaning Construction in Literature Study Groups." *In Research in the Teaching of English.* Vol. 23, No. 1 (1989).

Emmer, E., C. Evertson & L. Anderson. "Effective Classroom Management at the Beginning of the School Year." In *Elementary School Journal.* Vol. 80, No. 5 (1980).

Evertson, C. & E. Emmer. "Preventative Classroom Management." In *Helping Teachers Manage Classrooms* (D. Duke, Ed.).

Alexandria, Virginia: Association for Supervision and Curriculum Development, 1982.

Flanders, N. *Analyzing Teaching Behavior*. Reading, Massachusetts: Addison-Wesley, 1970.

Fontana, D. *Classroom Control: Understanding and Guiding Classroom Behavior*. London: Methuen, 1985.

Good, T. & J. Brophy. *Looking in Classrooms*, 4th Ed. New York: Harper & Row, 1987.

Jones, V.F. & L.S. Jones. *Comprehensive Classroom Management: Creating Positive Learning Environments*, 2nd Ed. Boston, Massachusetts: Allyn & Bacon, 1986.

Kounin, J. *Discipline and Group Management in Classrooms*. New York: Holt, Rinehart & Winston, 1970.

Newman, J. "Insights from Recent Reading and Writing Research and Their Implications for Developing Whole Language Curriculum." In *Whole Language: Theory in Use* (J. Newman, Ed.). Portsmouth, New Hampshire: Heinemann, 1985.

Parry, C. *Let's Celebrate: Canada's Special Days*. Toronto, Ontario: Kids Can Press, 1987.

Slavin, R.E. *Educational Psychology: Theory into Practice*. Englewood Cliffs, New Jersey: Prentice Hall, 1986.

Staab, C. "Teachers' Practices with Regard to Oral Language." In *The Alberta Journal of Educational Research*. Vol. 37, No. 1 (1991).

Talk Structures

Bianchi, J. *The Swine Snafu*. Newburgh, Ontario: Bungalo Books, 1988.

Bloom, B.S. *Taxonomy of Educational Objectives, Handbook I: Cognitive Domain*. New York: David McKay, 1956.

Brown, M. *Stone Soup: An Old Tale*. New York: Scribner's, 1947.

Dale, E. *Audio-Visual Methods in Teaching*, 3rd Ed. New York: Holt, Rinehart & Winston, 1969.

Graves, D. *Writing: Teachers and Children at Work*. Exeter, New Hampshire: Heinemann, 1983.

Johnson, D.W., R.T. Johnson & E.J. Holubec. *Circles of Learning: Cooperation in the Classroom*. Minneapolis, Minnesota: Association for Supervision and Curriculum Development Press, 1984.

Johnson, D.W. & R.T. Johnson. *Leading the Cooperative School*. Edina, Minnesota: Interaction, 1989.

Lindfors, J. *Children's Language and Learning*, 2nd Ed. Englewood Cliffs, New Jersey: Prentice Hall, 1987.

Slavin, R.E. *Cooperative Learning*. New York: Longman, 1982.

Functions of Language

Halliday, M. *Learning How to Mean: Explorations in the Study of Language*. London: Edward Arnold Press, 1975.

Rosen, C. & H. Rosen. *Language in Primary Classrooms*. London: Penguin, 1975.

Shafer, R., C. Staab & K. Smith. *Language Functions and School Success*. Glenview, Illinois: Scott, Foresman, 1983.

Tough, J. *Focus on Meaning: Talking to Some Purpose with Young Children*. London: Allen & Unwin, 1973.

Listening

Hoskisson, K. & G. Tompkins. *Language Arts Content and Teaching Strategies*. Toronto: Merrill, 1987.

Lundsteen, S.W. *Listening: Its Impact at All Levels on Reading and Other Language Arts*. Urbana, Illinois: National Council of Teachers of English, 1979.

Nessel, D., M. Jones & C. Dixon. *Thinking through the Language Arts*. New York: Macmillan, 1989.

Porat, K. "Listening, the Forgotten Skill." In *Momentum*. Vol. 21, No. 1 (1990).

Rankin, P. "The Importance of Listening Ability." In *The English Journal*. Vol. 17, No. 6 (1928).

Shoop, M. "Inquest: A Listening and Reading Strategy." In *The Reading Teacher*. Vol. 39, No. 7 (1986).

Stauffer, R. *Directing the Reading-Thinking Process*. New York: Harper and Row, 1975.

Stauffer, R. *The Language Experience Approach to Teaching Reading*, Revised Ed. New York: Harper & Row, 1975.

Temple, C. & J. Gillet. *Language Arts: Learning Processes and Teaching Practices*. Glenview, Illinois: Scott, Foresman, 1989.

Wilt, M.E. "A Study of Teacher Awareness of Listening as a Factor in Elementary Education." In *Journal of Educational Research*. Vol. 43, No. 8 (1950).

Wolvin, A. & C. Coakley. *Listening Instruction*. Annadale, Virginia: Speech Communication Association, 1979.

"Doing" Oral Language in the Classroom

Atwell, N. *In the Middle: Writing, Reading and Learning with Adolescents*. Portsmouth, New Hampshire: Boynton/Cook, 1987.

Zola, M. "I Bought Me a Cat." In *Good Morning Sunshine* from Impressions, Vol 4. (D. Booth and J. Phoenix, Eds.). Toronto, Ontario: Holt, Rinehart & Winston, 1984.